A Gringo Manual on How to Handle Mexicans

A Gringo Manual on How to Handle Mexicans

Second Edition, Revised and Expanded

José Angel Gutiérrez

Arte Público Press
Houston, Texas

This volume is made possible through grants from the National Endowment for the Arts (a federal agency), Andrew W. Mellon Foundation, the Lila Wallace-Reader's Digest Fund and the City of Houston through The Cultural Arts Council of Houston, Harris County.

Recovering the past, creating the future

Arte Público Press
University of Houston
Houston, Texas 77204-2174

Cover design by James Brisson

Gutiérrez, José Angel.
   A Gringo Manual on How to Handle Mexicans / José Angel
Gutiérrez.—2nd ed. rev. and expanded
      p.   cm.
   ISBN 1-55885-326-X (pbk. : alk. paper)
      1. Mexican Americans—Civil rights—Handbooks, manuals, etc.
   2. Civil rights movements—United States—Handbooks, manuals, etc.
   3. Mexican Americans—Civil rights—Anecdotes.   4. Civil rights
   movements—United States—Anecdotes.   5. United States—Ethnic
   relations—Handbooks, manuals, etc.   6. United States—Ethnic
   relations—Anecdotes.   I. Title.   II. Series.
   E184.M5 G87 2001
   323.1'16872073—dc21   2001022421
                                                               CIP

♾ The paper used in this publication meets the requirements of the American National Standard for Information Sciences—Permanence of Paper for Printed Library Materials, ANSI Z39.48-1984.

1 2 3 4 5 6 7 8 9 0   10 9 8 7 6 5 4 3 2 1

*To my mother, Concepción Fuentes Gutiérrez.
I know you would have enjoyed this version and probably
stashed a few hundred away for posterity. I miss you
and thank you for making me the man that I am.*

Table of Contents

Foreword

The 1960s and 1970s spawned some of the most significant Hispanic civil rights and social justice activities in U.S. history. During these years, Americans gained unprecedented exposure to the plight of Spanish-speaking people in the United States, through the organizing activities of Hispanic workers, students, artists, and community activists. Five leading figures emerged to embody the particular struggles for Mexican Americans. Their works informed the development of a national Chicano civil rights movement.

César Chávez, head of the United Far Workers Union, became the most well known of these leaders nationally. Bert Corona, a Los Angeles-based labor leader and immigrant advocate, played a key role in expanding the base and assertiveness of Hispanic urban advocacy in California. Reis López Tijerina, a New Mexico-based Pentecostal preacher, mobilized aggrieved Mexican-American families around increasingly militant efforts to reclaim land rights guaranteed by the 1848 Treaty of Guadalupe Hidalgo between the United States and Mexico, which in many cases had been blatantly violated. Rodolfo "Corky" Gonzales, a Denver-based community organizer, contributed a new conceptual framework to the Mexican-American struggle for justice, invoking the notion of a lost homeland—Aztlán—in powerful public addresses and writings that especially galvanized young activists of the day.

The last of these leadings figures was José Angel Gutiérrez. Gutiérrez, a young community and political organizer from South Texas, spearheaded a new vehicle to alter radically Mexican-American political participation: the Raza Unida ("United People's") Party. During the early 1970s, the Raza Unida Party succeeded against overwhelming odds to win key elected offices in and the South, thus help-ing to change the face of U.S. Hispanic politics in important ways.

Gutiérrez's political activities produced a substantial body of FBI surveillance and disapproving establishment scrutiny. The political movement that he helped to forge ultimately waned, as so many mod-ern American third-party efforts have. Gutiérrez persevered in the aftermath of the Raza Unida Party's demise to pursue a career as a lawyer and progressive scholar. He remained active in community affairs and organizing activities, developing a widely read under-ground book called *A Gringo Manual on How to Handle Mexicans,* which he self-published in the 70s. The volume presented here repre-sents substantial efforts by Gutiérrez to advance the quality, currency, and relevance of the manual (through constant editing and updating over the years), while simultaneously preserving the spirit and feel of the original.

We are pleased to present this key product of the Chicano Move-ment years as a leading release in Arte Público Press's Hispanic Civil Rights Book Series. The series seeks to increase public knowledge and appreciation concerning Hispanic contributions to U.S. civil rights advancement in the post-World War II era. With generous sup-port from the Charles Stewart Mott Foundation, the Rockefeller Foun-dation, and the Ewing Marion Kauffman Foundation, the series will support the public dissemination and discussion of approximately fif-teen new and revised works covering the key organizations and lead-ers that have shaped contemporary gains by Hispanics in social jus-tice. By pointing out the many public achievements of these groups and individuals, even in the face of substantial mainstream resistance, the series aims to expand national comprehension of the strength and vitality of U.S. democratic institutions, and of the promise of our nation's dramatically increasing cultural diversity.

José Angel Gutiérrez's *A Gringo Manual* presents lessons, most-ly quite humorous but in every case bitingly insightful, about the many daily injustices Mexican Americans and Mexican people encounter at the hands of white, North American "gringos" across the United States. Based on Gutiérrez's own personal experiences and insights, as well as those of other aggrieved people of Mexican origin, the entries in *A Gringo Manual* provide first-voice testimony to the continuing legacy of institutionalized racism in America. They underscore the conditions, assumptions, and biases that produced militancy in so many, especially younger Mexican Americans of the civil rights era.

As Hispanic Americans emerge to become the nation's most populous minority group at the outset of the 21st century, many of the injustices chronicled in Gutiérrez's *A Gringo Manual* sadly are on the rise. Mexican origin and other Hispanic Americans suffer continuing indignities at the hands of politicians, law enforcement officials, employers, universities, the media, philanthropic grant-making organizations, and other leading institutions. Hispanics and especially newer immigrants are also increasingly subject to the nation's growing incidence of racially motivated hate crimes. Gutiérrez's entries in *A Gringo Manual* bring forward in full-blown color the tragedy and the pettiness of contemporary anti-Latino racism, xenophobia, and institutional bias. They amplify the absurdity of still too prevalent mainstream perceptions of Mexican and other Latino people in the U.S. as lazy "foreigners" who are somehow undeserving of equal status in American life.

Quite importantly, however, Gutiérrez's introductory remarks in this important new volume make it clear that to be a "gringo" is not a condition of racial or ethnic assignment. Instead, he observes, to be gringo speaks to a state of mind—that is, a mind to be anti-Hispanic. Hence, in Gutiérrez's comprehension of the term, Mexican Americans and other Hispanics can also be gringos—and indeed many regrettably are. Conversely, not all European (or other non-Hispanic) Americans are gringos.

In effect, what Gutiérrez is suggesting here is that the continuing persistence of gringo-mindedness and gringo practice in America is neither preordained nor immune from the powerful influences of reason and social evolution. Americans of all backgrounds have the power and the opportunity to overcome our sad gringo legacy. We have the intellectual capacities to place our common humanity before our worst instincts and our darkest historical biases. The remaining unanswered question, however, is whether we finally have the vision and the will to do so.

The lifework of José Angel Gutiérrez, and this updated volume of *A Gringo Manual,* challenge us to address these fundamental issues. A leading protagonist of the Chicano Movement's heyday, Gutiérrez remains today a fiercely committed, though perhaps less visible and galvanizing community advocate. His large contributions to the political and intellectual struggle for Hispanic equality in America, however, will have long-enduring impacts. His place in the pantheon of progressive change agents in U.S. Latino history is secure. The work that follows reflects the reasons for this. Arte Público Press is privileged indeed to extend this important leader's contributions to the public record.

Henry A. J. Ramos

Acknowledgments

First of all, I thank the thousands of Chicanos, Chicanas, and others who have given me useful criticism and new information about power relations between Anglos and Chicanos and others to write this revised edition. These persons are too numerous to mention here, but you know who you are. And, I also thank the hundreds of you who kept asking for copies of the original version over the years and pressured me to complete the sequel. I also thank Nicolás Kanellos, founder and director of Arte Público Press, for indicating an interest in publishing this revised edition. He first mentioned his interest in a revised version when I was running in the 1993 special election to fill a United States Senate seat (Lloyd Bentsen's). Later, in 1998, when I was a Visiting Scholar at the University of Houston, sponsored by the Mexican-American Studies Program under the leadership of Dr. Tatcho Mindiola, Dr. Kanellos and I discussed this work, and a sequel, *The Chicano Manual on How to Handle Gringos,* over lunch. Soon, I had contracts in hand for several projects. Marina Tristán and Clifford Crouch, both of Arte Público Press, also provided encouragement, showed patience with my pace, and provided excellent editing suggestions.

During the spring 2000 semester I had a reduced teaching load thanks to Dr. Dale Story, chair of the Political Science Department at my university, and was able to finish a first draft of the revised manuscript. My former program coordinator at the Center for Mexican American Studies at the University of Texas-Arlington, Diana Flores, re-keyboarded the original edition into a digital file so that I could correct typos, grammar, and have the material in proper format to revise. Thank you, Diana. I also thank Tobías Durán and Marina

Cadena at the Center for Regional Studies of the University of New Mexico at Albuquerque for their support and encouragement during the summer of 2000. And as usual, my family has again patiently waited for me to finish this project. "One of many," as they always remind me. Gloria, Andrea, and Clavel, I love you.

Introduction

The history of how *A Gringo Manual on How to Handle Mexicans* came about has many twists and turns. The idea for such a book emerged in the course of my work while at the University of Texas in the mid-1970s for my doctoral dissertation. During the summer of 1974 I wrote my dissertation on a theory of Chicano community organization. At that time, there were no personal computers, much less laptops. The actual work had to be done manually on a typewriter from notes on paper and index cards. I had hundreds of pages of written notes and some two thousand index cards, each containing a valuable piece of information for my dissertation, such as a footnote, a citation, an idea, and the like. The final draft of my dissertation was typed in San Diego, California. Upon my return to Texas, I presented the draft to my dissertation committee as my final product. It was rejected. According to some members of my committee, portions of some chapters were not scholarly enough, particularly the section on power relations between Chicanos and Anglos. Some members insisted on a clear rooting of the material within the traditional paradigm of political science theory. At that time there were very few books or articles on the specific subject regarding Chicanos. Fortunately, I still had my written notes, the first draft and all the index cards. I began reworking the material with the hopes of satisfying my committee.

Once, while spending the weekend in San Antonio, Texas, during my monthly U.S. Army Reserve duty, my car was broken into in the parking lot of the old Mario's restaurant (now demolished). My personal effects were strewn around the car. Things were missing that I could not find in or near my car. I found my briefcase containing some of the material on power relations between Chicanos and Anglos opened and thrown behind the restaurant. Gone were many pages of my dissertation notes, index cards, and my address book. Not finding my index cards or the other written and typed material of the dissertation draft, I had to recreate the entire content of the manuscript. I did this on weekends at Garner State Park, north of Uvalde, Texas. To this day, I suspect police agents as being responsible for this break-in. During the late '60s, '70s, and '80s, and perhaps to this day, many Chicanos were targets of government surveillance. I had been under surveillance by federal and state government agencies because of my activities on behalf of the Chicano community. I have placed some FBI and CIA files on the surveillance pertaining to the Mexican American Youth Organization (MAYO), the Raza Unida Party, and me, on deposit with the University of Texas at San Antonio and at Austin.

My dissertation was on Chicano community organizing in a rural South Texas community, *Cristal*. The doctoral committee, however, again found some portions of the revised draft unacceptable. They claimed portions of the manuscript still lacked proper academic jargon and that some sections were void of in-depth political science analysis, particularly the Chicano-Anglo power relationships. What I had done in the section on power relationships was to list 130 anecdotal mini-stories about power and entitled the section "Gringo Tricks." The listings were true stories of experiences related to me by Chicanas and Chicanos that they had had with the Anglo power structure in South Texas and some experiences that I witnessed. I offered this as primary source and participant observer material. From my perspective in the light of scant material in the discipline, these anecdotes were both explanation and description of how the power relationships between Chicanos and the Anglo power structure played out. At that time I had difficulty with how to more fully incorporate and marry academic jargon to the material. I wanted to write my document in a way that my Raza could read and understand the plain English. I thought then that I could only analyze this asymmetrical relationship within the pages of my manuscript by presenting real and true cases as examples. The tricks would speak for themselves. While the dichotomy of power relationships between the "haves" (Anglos) and the "have-nots" (Chicanos) did not escape my attention in the writing, the analysis of this asymmetrical relationship and the specific theoretical underpinnings of such relationships did. I could not find many primary sources to cite, other than mine, nor could I find applicable secondary sources to support my contentions. The little work done in the area of power relations by such luminaries as Ernesto Galarza, Frantz Fanon, Carey McWilliams, Saul Alinsky, Manuel Gamio, Alonso Perales, Mancur Olson, Frances Piven and Richard Cloward, Rodolfo Acuña, Robert Blauner, and Eric Hobsbawn were not specifically on point. And few of these scholars—Galarza, McWilliams, Gamio, Perales, and Acuña—focused on the specific Chicano/Anglo power relationship in their works. I tried to avoid this problem by simply presenting this original material in a straightforward, clear, anecdotal format to my dissertation committee. It still was not in acceptable academic language to my committee. Exasperated, I turned to my senior adviser, Dr. Clifton McClesky, for advice on how to sidestep this problem and get my work approved by the committee. He simply said to me, "Leave it out. Make it an appendix." I did. The committee passed my dissertation favorably.

Later, Dr. McClesky suggested that I seek to have the appendix published by an academic press. He thought it was a clever way to broach the subject of power relationships, and that my writing style was humorous. I tried several publishers to no avail. The material was rejected as being too anti-gringo and not academic enough. This criticism continued into the future because of the use of the word gringo. On many occasions since then I've had to explain the word. The etiology is not of concern here, but I've used the word in the context of defining and identifying a person that is anti-Mexican, anti-Chicano, anti-immigrant in their attitude and outlook, and also bigoted, racist, nativist, and prejudiced against Raza, generally. Not all Anglos are gringos, and not all gringos are white. I have met some Hispanics, blacks, and Mexican nationals that are as racist and prejudiced against our Raza in the U.S. as any gringo. In fact, in Mexican society there is an entire class of anti-Mexican Mexicans. I have met many of them. And, I have met some Chicanos and Chicanas that are also anti-immigrant, particularly against Mexicans and Central Americans, our cultural cousins. The word gringo describes a mind-set in a person that upholds an ideological paradigm of superiority and also holds a racialized image of the poor as less worthy and subhuman—in this case, our Raza. The use of the word Raza similarly prompts questions. I use it here to mean people of Mexican ancestry, both Chicano people and Mexican nationals.

I finally looked into the costs associated with publishing the manuscript myself. Gene and Janie Monroe, both Anglos, of the Wintergarden Publishing House in Crystal City, Texas, helped me with understanding the process and costs of self-publishing. I found a printer in Piedras Negras, Coahuila, Mexico: Imprenta Velasco Burckhardt, S. A. And for a considerable amount less than what it would cost in the United States, I printed 20,000 copies.

I reworked the appendix into a manuscript and ended up with 141 different "tricks." Given the bargain exchange rate, I also translated the material into Spanish. The finished product became a bilingual text. Unfortunately, the printer in Piedras Negras, the border city across from Eagle Pass, Texas, changed many of my Chicano Spanish words to his version of a more proper Castillian Spanish. In other cases, the printer mistyped several English words. And so, the original book contained many typographical errors. I have corrected them in this revised work.

The next problem I encountered was in crossing the books into the United States. The quantity of books attracted the attention of the U.S. Customs officers inspecting goods coming across the United States-Mexico border. Books were dutyfree at the time. Upon physical inspection by opening a box, eyeing the provocative title and thumbing through the content of the book, the customs officers, however, became alarmed. They deemed the book to be subversive material and wanted to confiscate the entire load. I protested loudly. Ultimately, they refused me the importation of these books. I turned back my loaded pickup truck into Piedras Negras, Coahuila, Mexico, and resorted to other means of getting these books across the border. Days later, I finally succeeded in getting them across and delivered to my doorstep. Drugs, guns, and people are not the only things that cross the border "illegally." This experience convinced me that I should someday also write about how Chicanos are able to turn the tables on the monopo-listic and asymmetrical power relationship held by Anglos.

The arduous process of selling a book, originally priced at $2.50, began. *A Gringo Manual* was in print and in the hands of Chicanos and Chicanas even before my doctoral degree was conferred by the Univer-sity of Texas at Austin. I marketed the book at conferences and speak-ing engagements and with help by word of mouth of satisfied cus-tomers. In later years, my children would hawk them to conference participants and pocket the money. Today, in the spring 2000, Bolerium Books of San Francisco, and Tony Ryan, a bookseller in Washington, D.C., sell my book for $91 and $63, respectively, as a rare book.

Over the years the initial print run was exhausted. During the hey-day of the Chicano Movement, the decade of the '70s, this book became a vital reader for most Chicano activists. At many a meeting or presentation, I would be reminded by audience members that they had a comparable experience to an anecdote in *A Gringo Manual*. I have also been asked over the years when the sequel to this book will be published. For a long time I have felt that before work could begin on the sequel, *A Chicano Manual on How to Handle Gringos*, that *A Gringo Manual* had to be completely sold out. I thought that was the case toward the end of 1989, but I was wrong.

My mother died in September 1986 during my first year of law school. I could not bring myself to go and empty her home of her per-sonal belongings until years later. At the urging of my aunts on my mother's side, we finally went to remove those possessions in 1989. During this trip to Crystal City, Texas, I found a large box containing more than five hundred of the original books among her clothes in a closet. Why, how, or when she had put these books away is beyond me, but I'm glad to have these last remaining books. Many a friend of my mother has asked me from time to time to autograph his or her copy of *A Gringo Manual* that Conchita (my mother's nickname) had given them. I guess my mother relied on her stash of books for gifts to friends and acquaintances. Now, the books are almost gone. And, it is clear to me that it is time to not only revise *A Gringo Manual* but also to begin work on a sequel. This, then, is the first part of the task.

Part I of this book contains a brief essay on powerlessness that seeks to analyze the Chicano condition of powerlessness and identifies the gates out of it. Part II of this book contains new tricks. I have added another 100 such anecdotes to illustrate new and contemporary dimensions of the power relationship not previously explored in the original text. And in Part III, I include the English-language portion of the old manuscript with corrections to typographical and grammatical errors. The original book is out of print.

PART I

Powerlessness

Powerlessness is a condition that is imposed on people by the nature of the socioeconomic-political environment (system) in place. The powerless condition emanates from the system. Those in power, economic elites in the U.S. system, have an effective relationship between themselves and the environment—capitalism. Thomas Hobbes, many centuries ago, wrote in *Leviathan,* "The POWER of a man (to take it Universally,) is his present means, to obtain some future apparent Good" (MacPherson 1968: 150). In the case of the Chicano people, our powerlessness stems from the fact that we are denied access and blocked from developing a relationship with our capitalist environment. Capitalism requires wealth, particularly money, in order to effectively develop a relationship within the system. To operate within a capitalist system, a person needs money and access to more money with which to acquire the resources necessary to make the system respond. In our history, Raza has had little means available to obtain wealth and power.

We must learn to understand the nature and workings of the global capitalist system. Basically, capitalism feeds on the profits extracted from labor and profits extracted from consumption of goods and services. Raza, as all other people the world over, only have their labor to sell in the market. Few Raza are producers of goods and services. Even these few that do own their labor and hire others, do not also have influence or control over the marketing and distribution of their own products. Our Raza mini-capitalists fall prey to those that do control the market and distributions systems. Consequently, as a group of people, we have limited capital available, and our wealth is limited to little money and some ownership of property, usually a car or two and a home.

Let me review the origins and terms of our powerlessness.

The Origin and Terms of Powerlessness: Oppression

In the early nineteenth century, when whites overran the Mexican population in Texas, the condition of powerlessness was imposed. The first terms of the imposed condition were racial, demographic, and geographic. The whites, most who entered Texas and the Southwest without the sanction of the Mexican government, as illegal aliens, thought of themselves as superior beings and of Mexicans as inferior beings. Arnoldo De León (1983) traces the origin of Anglo attitudes in 1821 toward Mexicans in Texas up to the end of that century. De León posits that Anglos of the nineteenth century were more racist against their Mexican hosts than merely cultural chauvinists (p.xi). These early Anglo Texans thought Mexicans were their mental, physical, cultural, and moral inferiors. David Montejano (1987) expands on De León's foundation and traces the prevailing Anglo attitudes toward Mexicans in Texas from 1836, shortly after Anglo victory over Mexican President Santa Anna, to 1986. These racist attitudes are still held. In 1977, Douglas Foley et al, published their findings from a study of a South Texas community located in the Winter Garden area. He writes the early history of that community during the *Rancho* era, roughly the late 1800s to the middle-1930: "Ethnic relations during this era took place under an extremely exploitative, paternalistic sharecropper system and was supported by open racism, strict social segregation, and effective Anglo political machines" (p.xiii). These early Anglo attitudes were transplanted throughout the West and Southwest. Richard Baker, in a study of an Idaho community in the 1990s, writes, "Through their social interaction with one another and through the functioning of their social institutions, the Anglos had created and were sustaining a social system that implied that Mexican Americans are inferior to Anglos. This belief system had become a self-fulfilling prophecy that relegated and maintained Mexican Americans in a subordinate position in the community" (1995: vii). And

Dionicio Nodin Valdés (2000) traces the same patterns of white racism, segregation, discrimination and prejudice against Mexicans in the twentieth century throughout Midwestern cities.

White Texans and the African slaves they imported into the newly independent nation outnumbered Mexicans by 1836. By 1850 the black Texan population comprised 28 percent of the total population. Blacks in Texas maintained the numerical superiority over Mexicans until the early 1900s. In 1900, blacks were twenty percent of the population of Texas (Sharp 1992:10). From that period to the present time, Mexicans, in addition to being considered an inferior group, have also been dismembered as a people from their motherland, the Mexican culture and history. Mexicans have been outnumbered in their own land until recent times.

The Origin and Terms of Powerlessness: Anglo Hegemony

A second set of terms of the imposed condition was legal, economic, and cultural hegemony. Whites thought that the land and resources in the hands of Mexicans was going to waste and that it was their legal and moral duty to take and make use of this land and its resources for the benefits of whites only. Their white God predestined this legal and moral duty of white people, Manifest Destiny. And, they took the land of Mexicans and Native Americans.

The whites imposed their cultural mores and folkways on the society and made Mexican culture a segregated, undesirable way of life. Mexicans were killed by the thousands (Samora et al, 1979; Mirandé, 1987), and those left alive were run off their lands and into Mexico, including many Tejano Mexicans that had sided with the whites, such as Juan Seguín and Antonio Navarro. Texas became a state of the United States by 1850 and adopted the citizenship requirements then in place for the country. In 1790, the lily-white U.S. Congress (1857:184) had enacted "that all free white persons who have, or shall migrate into the United States, and shall give satisfactory proof before a magistrate, by oath, that they intend to reside therein, and shall take an oath of allegiance, and shall have resided in the United States for one whole year shall be entitled to the rights of citizenship." This first naturalization law had the effect of making the illegal Anglos (under Mexican rule) legal Texans, and therefore, first-class citizens. At the same time, notwithstanding the Treaty of Guadalupe Hidalgo that conferred U.S. citizenship on Mexicans if they remained in occupied Mexico, Mexicans were made "illegal aliens" and "immigrants." These labels remain in use today by the media, Anglo scholarship, and in legislation. Only after 1940 was the Mexican population officially classified by the U.S. Census Bureau as Caucasian; prior to that time Mexicans were classified as "Other Race" (Jacobson 1998.) In the last 2000 census, the Bureau allowed Raza to pick from four possible racial categories and umpteen ethnicities. This lack of control by Raza over their identity, racial and ethnic, only exacerbates the growing faultline for group solidarity.

The Origin and Terms of Powerlessness: Mexican Diasporas

The first of two Mexican Diaspora (1836 and 1848) came to pass. This first encounter between Mexicans and whites on Mexican soil became a self-fulfilling prophecy to whites. The Texas experience whetted their appetite for the rest of what is now the U.S. West and Southwest. The same scenario was repeated in 1850 in that geographic space. Since that time, whites have imposed a chronic condition on the Mexican people: underdevelopment that breeds poverty. The borderland, where most of the Mexican population continues to reside, is maintained underdeveloped. On the U.S. side of the border, the area is more a military zone than an industrial zone. The borderlands in every state—Texas, Arizona, New Mexico, and California—are a third-world country onto themselves. The socioeconomic and political indicators for the borderlands make this region the worst in the United States. This has been true since 1848 to the present time in Texas (Sharp 1998).

Once the region was politically incorporated as states into the American union, the last being New Mexico, a third set of imposed conditions was implemented. The third condition was political and institutional hegemony. The American capitalist system was imposed on the Mexican people via white institutions. In the schools the Mexican children were segregated and denuded of their culture as a prerequisite to learning the Anglo way. The purpose of the educational system is to make Anglos out of all children. Those Chicano children that refuse to conform and resist this cultural and psychological genocide are pushed out of the school system. Chicano children have the highest high school dropout rates of any ethnic/racial group. Angela Valenzuela in *Subtractive Schooling* (1999) provides the data to make this case. Access to higher education remains elusive for the Chicano people; less than .05 percent obtain doctoral or professional degrees. Rodolfo Acuña (1998), utilizing Thomas Kuhn's theory on paradigms in science, applied the concept to higher education. He concludes that Chicanos cannot access higher education because it is not designed with us in mind. The existing paradigm benefits white scholars over racial and ethnic scholars. The paradigm must be changed in order to obtain greater access. The Raza has a very limited pool of intellectuals and professionals.

In the labor arena, the Mexican people were made a reserve labor pool and exploitable due to immigration status. Mario Barrera in *Race and Class in the Southwest* (1979), among others early on, provided the data to make this case. Finally, at the beginning of the twenty-first century, organized labor began actively to seek resident and undocumented Mexican workers as members. Prior to this time, organized labor, like other institutions, rejected Mexicans as members. In the political arena, the Mexican people were effectively excluded from electoral power through various means until the mid-twentieth century. The ability to capture and hold public office by significant numbers of Chicanos and Chicanas did not occur until after 1975 with extension of the Voting Rights Act to Texas and other jurisdictions in the Southwest. The Mexican population is very young in age, with nearly half of the entire population under the age of eighteen and therefore ineligible to register to vote. Another 26 percent of the entire population are foreign-born and are not citizens. These persons are also ineligible to vote. The remaining 24–25 percent do register and vote but are not enough to form a majority in most localities, except the border counties. The potential political power of Mexicans in the electoral arena will reach apogee in the near future. In the government arena, as Alfredo Mirandé pointedly outlines in *Gringo Justice* (1987), the Mexican people were made the targets and objects of injustice rather than the beneficiaries and recipients of justice. In religious circles, the leadership of the Catholic Church surrendered its Mexican parishioners to Irish, German, French, Spanish, and Polish clerics, and removed the remaining Mexican priests and diocesan leaders. The people were left without the spiritual leaders who had been with them and had understood them. Access to health, education, culture, and travel was made cost-prohibitive, given the nature of the capitalist society imposed on Mexicans, and remains so to this day. There is no fundamental right under the U.S. Constitution to an education, to a curriculum, to a healthy life, to a job, or to "life, liberty, and the pursuit of happiness." The few cultural centers for Raza in major urban areas are recent constructs and depend on scarce resources and limited operational budgets. The *mutualista* organizations in rural areas that maintained and sponsored the cultural activities in those communities are rapidly disappearing. The Spanish-language media, while growing in recent decades, are not owned by Raza. A quick tour of any airport will reveal that the vast numbers of air travelers are white. These privileges can only be accessed with ample reserves of cash.

The System Does Not Work

A frequent lament heard from the mouths of Raza who feel they are victims of these conditions is that the system does not work. The capitalist system works very, very well indeed for most whites. The system was not designed for us or to benefit us. The system does allow for individual but not group ascendancy. The privileged group, whites, is in power. There is no room at the top for another group. There is always room for individuals from other nonwhite groups because such individuals can act as buffers, brokers, interlopers, tokens, and mediators between the white structure and Raza. By use of such a person, the system maintains its distance while at the same time channeling access and communication to itself via this person. If the issue at hand results in success for the whites, the intermediary is exalted and legitimized.

If the issue at hand results in disaster for the Raza, the broker is vilified and condemned by the Raza as a sellout, traitor, ineffective, etc. The whites, regardless, maintain a win-win situation while the Raza is fractured and divided by the use of these intermediaries.

Gates Out of Powerlessness

The powerlessness of Raza emanates from these conditions. To overcome these imposed and maintained conditions, Raza must transcend three levels, open three gates, if you will. First, the opening gate out of powerlessness is to learn how the world works. World is relative to time, space, learning, and experience. A child's world consists of family, household, neighborhood, school and school yard, city, and some other institutions such as church, youth groups (Little League, Girl Scouts, and the like), labor (paper route, migrant stream), business (neighborhood grocery, Wal-Mart, and 7-11s, for example), and social interaction with others. Too many of our children do not finish fully opening this gate; they are pushed out of school, targeted for harassment by authorities, particularly police, and made to enter the world of work before they completely exit the first gate and learn of the second gate. This Raza is functionally system-illiterate. They do not know how the world works, and because of this condition, they seldom access the system in any meaningful way for themselves or the group. Their condition of system illiteracy usually is passed on to their children. Worse yet, the offspring must operate without the assistance and advice of their parents.

The second gate out of powerlessness is for Raza to learn how to make the world work for them. In order to make the most of this arena, mentors, luck, and acquiring skills are essential. Luck is necessary because circumstances always limit the options a person has. Luck is that fleeting opportune moment that must be seized and used to change direction in life. Luck is opportunity—that sudden situation in which a decision must be made to pursue the unknown. Mentors are guides through this opportunity. A person must learn to recognize and seek a guide, and use both the mentor and the moment to reach a new level of understanding from one who has been in that situation before.

There are mentors constantly all around us. Mentors or guides are persons that, like you, give you advice (solicited or unsolicited), care for you, hire you, work with you, live with you, live down the street from you, take an interest in you, or simply answers your questions. But you must ask questions, the first being a request for help in understanding the situation. It is in this arena that Raza acquire and perfect personal skills, such as analytical and strategic thinking, public speaking, networking, accessing information, book knowledge, values and ethics, ideologies, philosophy, and planning. A few Raza high school and college graduates successfully operate at this level. The Raza middle class, by and large, is situated in this arena, and they are most comfortable with this station in life. This condition is satisfactory because there are rewards, mostly material and personal, such as earning a livable wage, comfortable housing with amenities, recreational time, and networks of similarly situated Raza and others. The illusion of inclusion into mainstream U.S. society is made real and affirmed daily for them. They do not view the capitalist system as a cause of Raza oppression; rather, it is viewed as a neutral framework that allows individuals, to reach levels where they can make the system work for them.

The last gate, which Raza seldom open and enter, is how to make the world. This arena requires recall of past experiences in the other two arenas and learning to put them into practice. Very few Raza ever attempt to maneuver in this arena.

Raza: Those That Watch, Wonder, and Do

Samuel P. Huntington (1981) clearly delineated the "ever-present gap . . . between American political ideals and American political institutions and practice" (p.4). He classified people, aware of this ever-present gap, into four broad categories: those that ignore, those that deny, those that tolerate, and those that try to eliminate the gap between what the promise of "democracy" ought to be and what it really is for racial and ethnic minorities. The first two categories of people are those that have an unclear perception of the gap and have a low intensity of belief in the ideals. The latter categories have a clear

perception of the gap and a high intensity of belief (p.64). The "elim-
inators" are the doers of the world. By attempting to close the gap
between ideals and reality, they make the world a better place for all.
To successfully make the world to one's liking, a person must learn
the relationship of power to the U.S. society; the role of an individual
in groups and society; one must have political consciousness; one
must know the depth of institutional power; and know how personal
and group interests are served by power. You must have acquired
extensive social capital with which to make fundamental social
change. Social capital, according to James S. Coleman (1990), is that
historical memory of what was; the ability to tap organizations and
people for resources; the mobilization of those resources toward tactics, strategy, and goal attainment; and leadership. Then, you must
take action. Those with social capital are the doers among us. The militant, activist, organizer, protestor, leader, advocate, rebel, radical, and
those that can channel rage into action are the doers that exercise cultural citizenship. William V. Flores and Rina Benmayor write that cultural citizenship is "a broad range of activities of everyday life
through which Latinos and other groups claim space in society and
eventually claim rights" (1997:15).

　　Not all Raza subscribe to the view presented here in this essay.
Others subscribe to various theories and hold contrary views—ideologies. It is the presence of these competing ideologies that negates
group solidarity. We do not all march to the same tune behind the same
drum major. There are many views of how the world works. Rodney E.
Hero (1992), among others, presents the dominant theories of how the
U.S. political system works and posits his own modification of the prevailing Anglo view: pluralism. Basically, he argues that Raza operate
on a lower level of the prevailing system. We are not the movers and
shakers of the system; the whites are. Only when we access and pene-
trate the upper level do Raza reach the ability to influence public policy and promote group interests. In essence, we are not in the white system, and whites do not need us to help them help themselves.

　　The lessons to be learned are clear: Remember what happened in
history; learn how the world works; become able to make the world
work for you; and make the world a better place for Raza.

References

Acuña, Rodolfo F. *Sometimes There Is No Other Side.* Notre Dame: University of Notre Dame Press, 1998.

Baker, David. *Los Dos Mundos: Rural Mexican Americans, Another America.* Logan, Utah: Utah State University Press, 1995.

Coleman, James S. *Foundations of Social Theory.* Cambridge: Harvard University Press, 1990.

De León, Arnoldo. *They Called Them Greasers: Anglo Attitudes Toward Mexicans in Texas, 1821-1900.* Austin: University of Texas Press, 1983.

Flores, William V. and Rina Benmayor. Eds. *Latino Cultural Citizenship: Claiming Identity, Space, and Rights.* Boston: Beacon Press, 1997.

Foley, Douglas E., Clarice Mota, Donald E. Post and Ignacio Lozano. *From Peones to Políticos: Class and Ethnicity in a South Texas Town, 1900-1987.* Austin: University of Texas Press, 1977.

Hero, Rodney E. *Latinos and the U.S. Political System: Two-Tiered Pluralism.* Philadelphia: Temple University Press, 1992.

Huntington, Samuel P. *American Politics: The Promise of Disharmony.* Cambridge: Belknap Press, 1981.

Jacobsen, Matthew Frye Jacobson. *Whiteness of a Different Color: European Immigrants and the Alchemy of Race.* Cambridge: Harvard University Press, 1998.

MacPherson, C.B. ed. *Leviathan.* Baltimore: Penguin Books, 1968.

Mirandé, Alfredo. *Gringo Justice.* Notre Dame: University of Notre Dame Press, 1987.

Montejano, David. *Anglos and Mexicans in the Making of Texas, 1836-1986.* Austin: University of Texas Press, 1987.

Samora, Julián, Joe Bernal and Albert Peña. *Gunpowder Justice: A Reassessment of the Texas Rangers.* Notre Dame: University of Notre Dame Press, 1979.

Sharp, John. *The Changing Face of Texas.* Austin: Comptroller of Public Accounts, 1992.

___. *Bordering the Future: Challenge and Opportunity in the Texas Border Region.* Austin: Comptroller of Public Accounts, 1998.

U. S. Congress. *Annals of Congress, Vol. 1, Abridgements of the Debates of Congress, 1789-1856.* New York: D. Appleton and Company, 1857.

Valdés, Dionicio Nodin. *Barrios Norteños: St Paul and Midwestern Mexican Communities in the Twentieth Century.* Austin: University of Texas Press, 2000.

PART II

A Gringo Manual on How to Handle Mexicans

New and Revised Version

1. Obituary

Carlos Guerra, a columnist for the *San Antonio Express-News*, told me that when César Chávez died, he spoke to the managing editor of the newspaper about running the notice of this leader's death on the front page, complete with a fuller story on his many accomplishments and the struggle to build a union of farm workers. Carlos thought the news warranted greater exposure than an obituary piece. The managing editor supposedly replied, "We don't run obits on the front page." Undaunted, Carlos sought out Dino Chiecchi, then a regional vice-president of the National Association of Hispanic Journalists (NAHJ), who also worked at the newspaper, to press the managing editor for front-page coverage of César's death. Dino went into the editor's office and was told, "No. I've already told Carlos that." Dino, as he came out of the office, turned to Carlos and said, "Well, buddy, I tried."

Chicanos and Chicanas in leadership positions need to be more assertive, not take "no" for an answer, and demonstrate solidarity with the task at hand (and the larger agenda as well).

2. "Macho"

The white, woman attorney was presenting a seminar on "Sexual Harassment on the Job Site" to lawyers attending a continuing legal education (CLE) training course. Lawyers across the nation are required to take a varying number of hours of these CLE courses to remain in good standing with the bar association. Throughout the first half-hour of the presentation, she kept using the word "macho" to describe an attitude of male dominance, behavior, and demeanor that constituted sexual harassment in the workplace. She always said "macho," never any other words, such as sexist, chauvinist, anti-woman, etc., to refer to a perpetrator of sexual harassment.

I protested her use of the word in Spanish because the inference implicit in "macho" was that all Spanish-speaking males were such. She disagreed. She promptly called on the audience members to vote by raising their hands to indicate support for her view or mine. She won by a landslide. The audience was white, mostly female, and it wholeheartedly agreed with her word choice and implication. Even the Hispanic lawyers in attendance supported her use of "macho" as the word to capture the essence of sexual harassment. So much for learning new aspects of the law. It is better to repackage old stereotypes as new material and keep Spanish-speaking males as potential sexual perpetrators.

3. Celebrating Brutality, Rape, Thievery and Outright Murder

Héctor A. Chavana, Jr., president of Movimiento Estudiantil Chicano de Aztlán (MEChA) at the University of Houston-Central Campus, wrote a letter to all interested organizations and individuals about protesting the yearly celebration held at the University billed as "Frontier Fiesta." This event commemorates the Anglo victory at San Jacinto over Mexicans in Texas in March 1835. Confederate flags are flown by groups in attendance, and Manifest Destiny has been the main topic of many speakers. At one such event held in April 1995, MEChA invited Raúl Salinas to read poetry and Evangelina Vigil-Piñón to sing in protest to the racist celebration. In counter-protest, the Anglo promoters of Frontier Fiesta upped their loud-speakers and drowned out both of the Chicano artists. Now, MEChA holds a candlelight vigil at Lynn Eusan Park as counter-protest to Frontier Fiesta. Question: Is it ethically sound for students at a public university to celebrate the murder, rape, and destruction of Mexicans?

4. No Benefits

Chicanas in the Yakima Valley of the state of Washington work year-round in refrigerated buildings, called "coolers," processing vegetables. They work for minimum wages without the usual benefits afforded other workers. The state authorities in complicity with the owners of these "coolers" have classified these workers as seasonal agricultural workers, just like migrant workers. The definition, however, exempts these workers from the standard and usual fringe benefits afforded other workers. Yet, they are not migrant agricultural laborers; they continue to live in the Yakima Valley year in and year out. Those who define, rule.

5. Welfare Reform

President Clinton, acting like a Republican, signed legislation requiring persons on welfare, mostly women of color with children, to attend retraining education and go back to work or they will be dropped from public assistance. Thousands and thousands of women and children are off the welfare rolls despite having attended retraining sessions. There are few jobs available to these persons that pay a living wage. On the other hand, cash money from the government to the private sector is not considered welfare when it flows to the tobacco industry, white widows on Social Security survivor's benefits, bail out of the savings-and-loan moguls, crop subsidies, cash incentives to place land in soil conservation programs, advertising costs for companies selling products abroad, the Overseas Private Insurance Corporation (OPIC), and the age-old oil and gas depletion allowance. Those that define, always win.

6. Three Strikes and You're In

A few years back, Ramsey Muñiz, the Raza Unida Party candidate for governor in 1972 and 1974, was charged and convicted of a third felony. President Clinton and the U.S. Congress had passed a new crime bill that made three felony convictions grounds for the imposition of a life sentence. Ramsey is in for life. Meanwhile, his wife and supporters are attempting to reopen the case and investigate the facts surrounding this third offense. To them, Ramsey is a political prisoner. To Clinton and company, Ramsey is a three-time loser. Besides, the United States has no political prisoners, Clinton and company argue.

7. Three DWIs and You're Outta Here

The Immigration and Naturalization Service (INS), better known in Raza circles as "La Migra," recently announced a new dragnet to deport unwanted persons of Mexican ancestry. If a person not yet a U.S. citizen is convicted of three Driving While Intoxicated (DWI) offenses in Texas, INS will hunt down and deport that person. It matters not that others with the same number of DWIs, who are citizens, will not be hunted much less deported. It matters not that for each offense, both the citizen and the not-yet-a-citizen have fully paid fines and court costs, served their time in jail, and perhaps had their driving licenses suspended for a period of time. The latter will be deported. It matters not that the time span for the three convictions goes back ten or more years; it's the magic number of three that counts. Isn't punishment for retroactive offenses prohibited by the ex post facto clause in the First Amendment, Section 9, Paragraph 3, of the U.S. Constitution?

8. Racemandering

Governor Elbridge Gerry of Massachusetts in 1812 developed a neat way, gerrymandering, to exclude his political enemies from voting against him. He removed them from the district in which he was running and thereby made them ineligible to vote in his election. Gringos and other rednecks picked up this trick with fervor and applied it to deny minorities the structural opportunity to elect someone of their choice. With passage of the Voting Rights Act (VRA) in 1965 and subsequent amendments and extensions of this law, at-large elections and gerrymandering became illegal acts. Minority voters brought lawsuits alleging vote dilution, gerrymandering, and use of at-large elections as means to keep them from winning. Minority districts were created, and minority voters proceeded to elect representatives of their choice, usually someone that looked like them and was one of them. Along came the Ronald Reagan era, and the U.S. Supreme Court took a second look at this new window of opportunity for minorities. In the case of *Shaw v. Reno* (1995), the high court ruled that race could not be utilized to draw a district. What whites had been doing before the VRA was passed and implemented has become illegal again. It's okay to dilute minority voting strength. It is not okay to dilute white power.

9. Barely Won or Won Without a Runoff Election?

Freshman city council member for the city of Dallas Steve Salazar, the youngest person to win election to that body, made front-page news with his victory. The news report, however, tried to minimize the historic importance of this Chicano victory. The article in *The Dallas Morning News* of May 4, 1997, read, "But freshman member Steve Salazar of Oak Cliff survived a scare, warding off two challengers with just over 50 percent of the vote." Not only did Mr. Salazar win decisively with more than half of the votes cast in his favor, but also against all challengers, negating a need for a runoff election. I guess it is how you look at any election in which a Chicano wins: he barely won against everybody in the race . . .

10. Crossover Rage

Back when it was not cool to have a real Chicano name if you were a struggling recording artist or an aspiring movie star, you changed your name: Freddy Fender, Vicki Carr, Raquel Welch, Martin Sheen, Rita Hayworth, for example. Now, it's okay to have a Chicano name, even if you are an artist, but the rage is to cross over music formats and sing in English, leaving behind the music and fans that brought you success. Our brown music sound in the Southwest has gone from *Onda* music to *Chicano* music to *Tejano* music. The powers that be in the music industry have successfully compartmentalized and regionalized our music. I wonder if our music is called *Tejano* music in California or Illinois? Do we even have a music format of our own anymore? Perhaps, it is *salsa*.

11. Reverse Racism

If you're pro Chicano, you are perceived to be and labeled anti-gringo. Don't fall for this verbal trick of gringo jujitsu by being labeled a reverse racist. Being proud of your heritage, your identity, your persona, is very natural and expected. If you're not proud of yourself and if you don't like yourself, why should anybody else? You are expected to protect and promote your own interests.

12. Political Dollars for Democrats

While the lieutenant governor of Texas Robert "Bob" Bullock was in office, he collected hundreds of thousands of dollars from top administrators within the University of Texas System. From the president at every university within the University of Texas System down to the dean level, he solicited or had someone solicit contributions for his political campaigns. Often the president of each constitution would be the head fundraising cheerleader. They gave thousands of dollars to this candidate. Yet, if any other individual that works for state government solicits money for partisan, political candidates, she or he may get fired. You can even get fired for refusing to give a donation under these circumstances. If you don't believe me, ask Jude Valdez, a former vice-president at the University of Texas at San Antonio, who refused his president a donation to Bullock and was subsequently demoted from his position. He had to sue the university to get his job back.

13. Contract with State

After my first lawsuit against the University of Texas at Arlington ended with a settlement agreement, which called for the purchase of books about Mexican-Americans for the main library, among other settlement terms, a committee was formed with me as its chair. Our committee proceeded to establish a process whereby interested faculty would take their recommendations and proceed to recommend books for purchase and acquisition. The university president saw fit to circumvent this process and instructed the general librarian to buy any and all books and exhaust all funds as quickly as possible. The head librarian and his staff proceeded to order as many books as the money would allow within a record time over the 1996-1997 Christmas holidays. Our committee and I were bypassed completely. When I sued for breach of the settlement agreement, my attorneys and I began the process of discovery that revealed the president's interference with the process. Shortly thereafter, the attorneys for the university smugly told me that in order to sue the university president as an agent for the state, I would have to get the state legislature to grant me permission via a legislative resolution. Not only did I get a resolution introduced but also immediately taken under consideration by an appropriate committee. The university raised the white flag, and we entered into a second settlement agreement. The point is: Do not waive liability from the opposing side in any contract agreement involving a representative of the state; otherwise, you may have to get a resolution passed by the state legislature to sue.

14. Plea Bargain

Approximately 95 percent of all criminal cases filed in Texas are settled by plea bargain. It is a bargain in the criminal justice process when the defendant and the state negotiate the punishment and fine in lieu of a trial. If you're charged with an offense, the state prosecutor may recommend, for example, two years' jail time probated for five years, plus court costs. There are different kinds of probation—straight and deferred adjudication. Under straight or deferred probation, if you commit another crime during the probationary period, your probation is revoked, and if you are convicted of the new offense, you will serve the original two-year term and whatever new time is added for the second offense. Be sure you opt for deferred adjudication if you qualify. In order to qualify, you must not have a criminal record. The good thing about deferred adjudication is that after you successfully complete your probationary period, the case record is removed in Texas.

15. Mr. Kimmel's Cultural History

In a recent book by Michael Kimmel, *Cultural Man in America* (New York: The Free Press, 1996), he attempts to write a cultural history of man. He describes the experience of men in America as that of the "self-made" man. They had absolutely no help from anyone in reaching their goals. But Chicanos are not described in this book. What is the message? One, Chicanos are not men. Two, Chicanos have no history in America. Three, Chicanos made no contribution.

And fourth, Chicanos were invisible, at least to Michael Kimmel and the publisher, The Free Press.

16. Cultural Disease

In recent publications in the health field, many writers define certain illnesses as culturally based. For example, it's not unusual to find an article about the overincidence of sickle cell anemia found among African-Americans. Nor is it unusual to find AIDS among drug users, prostitutes, promiscuous persons, and homosexuals. In the case of Chicanos, these health researchers describe our diseases to be predominantly diabetes, hypertension, and obesity. Is it the culture? I think it is the poverty, substandard housing, the illiteracy, no health insurance, no access to health care, the diet, the stress from assimilation, and the like. What do you think? Are we born defective?

17. Identity

In 1980, many news accounts and human-interest stories picked up the advertising hype that we were entering "the decade of the Hispanic." Accordingly, the U.S. Bureau of the Census utilized that term as a catchall to subsume all ethnic groups that shared Spanish-based "Hispanic ancestry." To be sure, it was not indigenous or mestizo-based origin—rather, some Spanish connection. As persons of Mexican ancestry, we should have a problem with this. Again in 1990, the U.S. Census Bureau utilized the term Hispanic to classify all groups and added four racial categories of Hispanics: black, white, brown, and yellow. In its functional form, the term Hispanic hides Mexicans. If an issue is raised peculiar to persons of Mexican ancestry, that "unrecognized" group has a problem but not Hispanics. The term is a generic label applied to everyone at the same time and therefore to no one. Yet again, in the 2000 U.S. Census enumeration, the bureau not only used the four-race-pronged category but added a mixed-race dimension. And we have encountered the problem: The official group name for all of us is Hispanic; there is no Chicana or Chicano allowed as a classification. You can pick Latino or Latina.

18. Latino or Latina—to Be or Not to Be?

Many Chicanos and Chicanas, in order to protest being labeled Hispanic, proudly proclaim themselves to be Latinos. Well, the terms Latina/o are not of Spanish origin but French, emanating during the era of Napoleon III and his subsequent invasion of Mexico in 1859-60. Is it still not a European term that ignores our mestizo and indigenous origins?

19. Concealed Weapons

In Texas, for decades, a person has been able to carry a weapon if it is in plain view and not concealed on his person or vehicle. Think of the many ranchers and wannabe cowboys that you have seen with their rifles plainly visible, racked across the back windshield of their pick-ups. In the late 60s and early 70s, members of the Black Panther party in Oakland, California, sported shotguns while policing the police. Apparently, California at that time had a law similar to that of Texas. Today in Texas, you can also carry a concealed weapon. The largest numbers of applicants for these permits are Anglo men residing in West Texas. Anglo Texans must feel threatened more than we do. I wonder why?

20. Illegality

I ran in the special election for United States senator from Texas in 1993. One of the candidates during this election was Congressman Fields, a Republican from Humble, Texas. In the course of the campaign, we had several debates among the top six candidates, of which I was one. At a first debate, Congressman Fields referred to Mexicans without documents as "illegal aliens." After that one debate, I asked him not to use the term and suggested he use undocumented persons or persons without U.S. citizenship. At the next debate, he again used "illegal aliens." This time, however, I was prepared for a second slip of the tongue and, as soon as he uttered them, pitched a T-shirt with the words "Superman is an illegal alien" on it. That portion of the T-shirt landed squarely on his face before the television cameras. He never did that again. Thereafter, all the candidates agreed that the only illegal aliens we have are Mighty Mouse, Wonder Woman, Superman, Spider Man, Elastic Man, and E.T.

21. He Can't Win . . .

Mexican-American Democrats is a political organization that seeks to promote, support, and endorse any Mexican American seeking public office in Texas. In 1996, a candidate by the name of Victor Morales ran in the Democratic primary seeking the nomination for United States senator. He was running against various Anglo candidates, most of whom were congressmen. The traditional Mexican-American Democrat leaders, such as Henry B. Gonzales (D-San Antonio), said Morales did not stand a chance and supported one of the Anglo candidates. Other Mexican-American leaders did the same thing and endorsed the favorite liberal, Congressman John Bryant, in that race. The Chicano voters' bloc voted for Victor Morales. Chicanos cast 48 percent of the votes within the Democratic Party primary election. The declining Anglo Democrats in Texas, only 26 percent, split their votes among the other four white males. The outcome was predictable: Morales won the highest voter percentage and entered into a run off election with John Bryant. And Morales beat John Bryant in the runoff election. Morales became the first Mexican-American Democratic candidate for the U.S. Senate in the November general election. But Chicanos are only about 16 percent of the total Texas vote, and Morales lost in the general election to the incumbent Republican Senator Phil Gramm.

22. Military Votes

If you're in the U.S. military, you can register to vote anywhere in any of the states, regardless of residence. In Del Rio, Texas, a border community in Val Verde County, there is a military installation, Laughlin Air Force Base, with personnel from all over the world. In the 1996 election, two former Anglo military persons became local Anglo candidates for county office as sheriff and county commissioner against local Chicanos. The Anglos won. One formerly was the founding member of a Ku Klux Klan chapter in Germany and the other was a similarly shady character, both Republicans. Their votes came from outside the county, mostly from military bases in Germany, cast by military personnel they had served with in years past. These voters had never been in Del Rio, much less intended to live there upon retirement. This is a neat trick! Join the military and vote anywhere you want. Organize the troops, Raza!

23. Political Math

Political math is different than regular math. Ten plus ten does not necessarily equal twenty. For example, if you have ten votes and the other candidate also has ten votes, but you can switch five votes from her side to yours, now she only has five votes and you have fifteen. How many votes does it take for her to beat you? Not five, not ten, but at least eleven! So the political messages are clear: (1) Register new voters; (2) Switch existing voters; and (3) Keep track of how many votes you really need to win. For every one you lose, go find two more.

24. Raza Undercount

The 2000 census will again report an undercount of Raza population. In 1990 the undercount for Raza was about 5 percent of 23,000,000 or 1.5 million persons not accounted for. Why? First, the census forms are mailed, and that favors those with permanent homesteads. Raza has a low incidence of home ownership. Second, Raza does not trust the government sending questionnaires and people knocking on doors asking dangerous questions about such subjects as citizenship. Third, our people move around a lot. The census form does not catch up to us, and the census personnel won't find us. Many are still migrants, homeless, young, and illiterate. Fourth, the outreach programs were underfunded and seldom conducted in Spanish. The first letters announcing the beginning of the census process were sent out in English. A reference at the bottom of the letter directed you to Spanish on the reverse side and had instructions to call a tollfree 1-800 number for Spanish assistance. You had to read in English to know you could get help in Spanish, and the telephone number had umpteen other numbers to punch before you could get to the *español*. Fifth, the Census Bureau did not hire enough persons as enumerators, particularly Spanish speakers. Lastly, the Congress insisted and the Supreme Court ruled that the Census Act (Title 13, USC) mandated a physical headcount, known to undercount population, over statistical sampling, which increases the accuracy of the headcount.

For every person missed by the U.S. Census Bureau, some $5,600 federal dollars are lost. You do the math of 1.5 million missed Raza in 1990, times $5,600.

25. Political Allocation of Power

The Census Bureau's report on population numbers is not only used to allocate federal dollars to states for services, programs, infrastructure, and the like, but is also used to reapportion the 435 congressional seats. Roughly, every 500,000 persons should constitute a congressional seat. If we lost 1.5 million Raza persons in the 1990 enumeration, we technically lost three additional congressional seats.

26. Crack Them!

Reapportionment of population for redistricting purposes from Congress, to state legislatures, county government, municipalities, school and community college districts, and some judicial districts occurs every ten years beginning in years ending with one. Despite the problems of underrepresentation caused by the undercount for Raza, we have an additional problem if Democrats are in control of the legislative body doing the reapportionment and redistricting. The Democrats historically have taken the Raza community, as well as other racial and ethnic minorities and poor people, generally, and cracked that population base into as many pieces as they could so that each piece of population becomes a safe harbor for a Democrat. The majority of Raza vote for candidates of the Democratic Party—that is to say, our community is cracked into various districts to help reelect incumbent Democrats. And, the majority of elected Democrats are not Raza.

27. Pack Them!

The Democrats are not the only bad guys in the reapportionment and redistricting power plays. The Republicans historically have taken the opposite tack. They support plans to pack all the Raza population and other minorities into one or two districts. In this manner, they can reduce the number of safe harbors for Democrats and open more possibilities for Republicans. The trade-off for some aspiring Raza politicians is that they get to be the token or the first one in that office; so they support the Republican plan. These "one and onlys" argue that it is better to get one than none. Does the old Raza adage of "*Nos dan atole con el dedo*" fit this scenario?

28. Shoot the Villain!

Walt Disney Company made a ton of money with the film *Toy Story*. So it made a sequel and, in association with Activision (Santa Monica, California), produced the video game *Toy Story 2*. This video game had a Mexican character replete with a huge sombrero, bullet bandoleers, big mustache, etc. In order to advance to the next level in the game, the player had to shoot and kill the Mexican bandido.

Oscar de la Torre, a counselor at Santa Monica High School, thought the game was promoting virtual genocide of Mexicans with this character. He and others protested last December 1999, outside Activision headquarters. Walt Disney Company, the family entertainment icon, does not like negative publicity. The game had to be re-done without the offending Mexican bandido. Is it any wonder that real gringos kill real Mexicans along the border?

29. Kill the Mexicans!

Remember James Oliver Huberty? He's the fellow that shot and killed twenty-two Mexicans at a McDonald's in San Ysidro, California, in 1984. The gringo ranchers along the U.S.-Mexico border have gone on a killing rampage once again. On May 13, 2000, near Del Rio, Texas, rancher Sam Blakewood shot and killed Eusebio Haro

Espinoza of Guanajuato, Mexico, with a .357 Magnum "because Mr. Espinoza was passing through my ranch. That is trespassing." Richard Scott Baumhammers, a lawyer, also went on a killing spree of Mexican immigrants recently.

In Cochise County, Arizona, also on May 13, 2000, various white, anti-Mexican hate groups, and individuals joined in coalition, among them Glenn Spencer, leader of Voices of Citizens Together and American Patrol, Barbara Coe, Roger Barnett, and other vigilante ranchers. The purpose of the meeting was to organize them to conduct citizens' arrests of Mexican undocumented workers crossing their ranches. They publicly stated that they would "kill Mexicans if it becomes necessary." The KKK at this coalition meeting proposed placing anti-personnel land mines along the border. At this writing, no federal agency is investigating these extremist, white hate groups.

Near Brownsville, Texas, on May 21, 2000, a border patrol agent shot a young Mexican male in the upper chest, and he died. The FBI is handling the investigation. And these killings are a fraction of those reported in the media.

30. Making History

Usually, the states are the entities that carry out the death penalty. The U.S. government has not executed a federal prisoner in almost four decades. On August 5, 2000, Juan Raúl Garza, an accused marijuana smuggler and convicted killer, was to be executed and would have become the first federal prisoner in this century to be executed. The punishment was stayed by President Bill Clinton, however, pending a review of death row inmates. Critics of capital punishment, among other arguments, claim that minorities are over-represented among the ranks of those to be executed. To be exact, there were 17 minorities among the 19 federal inmates pending execution when Juan Raúl Garza was finally put to death by lethal injection on June 19, 2001. He followed Timothy McVeigh by just a few days and was executed in the same chamber in Terra Haute, Indiana.

Hey, we are making history in all kinds of ways.

31. They Looked Mexican

Police agents have utilized racial profiling for decades. If you look Mexican (whatever that is), that is justification enough for a law enforcement agent to pull you over and demand identification. Gov. Gray Davis (D-California) finally agreed to support legislation banning race profiling in his state. In 1999, he vetoed similar legislation saying, "There is no evidence that this practice is taking place statewide." Well, the San Jose Police Department, which was collecting data on the incidence of racial profiling as justification for law enforcement stops, found that Raza and blacks were pulled over in greater percentages than they were represented in the population. And, the problem was so egregious that the U.S. Court of Appeals for the 9th Circuit ruled the practice of detaining persons on the basis of "Mexican appearance" while crossing at border checkpoints was unconstitutional. Besides, many California counties, such as Imperial County, have substantial Raza populations (73 percent). Accordingly, Hispanic appearance is of little or no use in determining which particular individuals should be detained by the border patrol on the lookout for undocumented persons.

Do you think the practice of racial profiling in search of illegal Canadians would work? Maybe the problem of determining which white persons were illegally crossing that border would be too difficult an undertaking.

32. The Battle at Seattle

Raza organizations, groups, and individuals were conspicuously absent from the protests aimed at the World Trade Organization Conference held in Seattle, Washington, in the spring 2000, and again during the protests against the World Bank and the International Monetary Fund held in Washington, D.C., during April 2000. Some Raza groups still hold the view that environmentalists also practice racism against our people because they seldom speak out against toxic dump locations, industrial plants in or near barrios, overdevelopment and excessive pollution in our geographic spaces.

MEChA in California voted to protest the Democratic Party National Convention held in Los Angeles during August 14–17, 2000. Other Raza groups invited to participate in the protests called "The Battle of Los Angeles," were the Brown Berets of Aztlán, Committee for Raza Rights, the Organization for the Liberation of Aztlán, and the Brown Beret National Organization. The reasons for the protests were that the Democrats have taken us for granted, continue to misrepresent Raza interests, are no different from the Republicans, and they recruit and help elect "vendido políticos" over genuine Raza grassroots leaders.

The real test of the protests was to see if enough Raza would participate and whether Raza Democrats would cross the picket lines and enter the convention hall. At this convention, however, there were more Raza Democratic delegates than ever, and the National Convention's chief executive officer was Lydia Camarillo, a Chicana originally from El Paso. The protest did not work.

33. NAFTA Braceros

Along with the passage of North American Free Trade Agreement (NAFTA), there emerged a new Bracero Program. Superior Forestry, operating in President Clinton's home state of Arkansas, recruited some two hundred Mexican workers from the state of Oaxaca. They were young indigenous men, mostly illiterate, from rural villages in that state. Their pay is $20 for every 1,000-pine seedling they plant in the mountains. Superior Forestry is but one company that has imported Mexican labor under NAFTA provisions. And like the old Bracero Program, 1940–1964, these workers have meager pay with no benefits. Food, transportation, clothing, personal toiletries, supplies, and equipment are deducted from their salaries. Some of them owe money to their employer, simply because they must eat and sleep seven days a week, and work may not be available seven days a week due to rain, cold, etc.

Can you believe we still have legalized slavery in the United States?

34. Earned Amnesty

A provision in the 1986 Immigration Reform and Control Act (IRCA) provided amnesty for persons who had been in the United States prior to 1981. They could apply for amnesty, obtain a "green card," and then apply for residency status in subsequent years. On May 4, 2000, the Senate Immigration Subcommittee held hearings on a new guest worker program (read Bracero). A provision in the current bill (S. 1814 and S. 1815) calls for earned amnesty. If a person has worked 150 days in agriculture prior to enactment of these bills, he or she could apply for earned amnesty, provided he continues to work another 180 days for five out of the next seven years before being eligible to apply for a green card (H-2A visa). The cruel hoax is that farm workers in 1997 and 1998 averaged 129 days of work per year. And, the number of farm jobs is decreasing.

Who benefits from this legislation? Growers, not farm workers.

35. Online Voting

Raza voters comprised 5 percent of the electorate in 1996 and nearly 8 percent in 2000. We are an emerging voting bloc that is of great interest to the major political parties and their candidates. Yet, the stereotype persists that Raza does not vote in sufficient numbers. The reality is we can't vote. About half of our population is under-age, another 26 percent are not citizens, and only 24 percent are eligible. Most of these do vote.

During the March 2000 primary in Arizona, the state conducted voting online. It was touted as a great success, and other states, such as California, New York, Florida, and Washington, are contemplating its use by 2004.

You can bet that the stereotype that Raza does not vote will continue. Has anybody figured out that you need a computer and access to the Internet before you can vote online? Raza households lag in ownership of personal computers and Internet access, compared to other minorities and, of course, whites. The statistics of those households with Internet access as of July 9, 1999, according to the U.S.

Commerce Department: 36 percent of Asians, 29.8 percent of whites, 11.2 percent of blacks, 12.6 percent of Hispanics.

36. Late Figures

The U.S. Census Bureau is scheduled to release preliminary population figures on April 1, 2001. These figures will show a tremendous population gain for Raza. This means that our population group will be entitled to more seats in all types of local governmental entities, such as cities, counties, school, and community college boards. Unfortunately, many cities, such as Dallas, Texas, will hold municipal elections on May 5, 2001. Not much time to get the official numbers and comply with the constitutional mandate to redistrict city council districts in time for the election—less than thirty-five days! More importantly, candidates for the Dallas city council must file for office by February 19, 2001. How are the interested candidates going to know in which district to file when the lines have not even been drawn, or if they even live in the "new" districts? Some officials are already talking about using old districts and setting up the new districts for the 2003 elections. They argue, that option would be better than facing litigation to stop elections for failure to redistrict in time and/or have special elections on other dates during the summer months.

Another option is to use the population numbers that have been scientifically adjusted to overcome the undercount, which would be legally permissible because the U.S. Supreme Court ruling did not preclude the use of statistical sampling numbers for purposes other than congressional seats. Regardless, lawsuits will fly, and Raza will have to wait to get more representation.

37. Right Place at the Right Time

Our votes are important, as is our geographic location, because we reside and vote in states that hold 85 percent of the electoral votes necessary to win the presidency. We are a growing power in some states; for example, in New Mexico we are 28 percent of the voting list, but this state only has five electoral votes. In four states we are very important: in New York we are 7 percent; in Texas 17 percent; in Florida 12 percent; and in California 11 percent.

38. Broken Promises

Spain was the first to grant land for homesteading to Anglos from the United States. Mexico, after independence from Spain in 1821, honored those agreements and gave even more land grants to Anglos, on three conditions: (1) loyalty to Mexico, (2) only Catholic could immigrate, and (3) no slaves were allowed. The first Anglos that came kept the promises, temporarily. Then came the gringo illegal aliens from Kentucky, Georgia, Tennessee, Alabama, the Carolinas, and Louisiana, in droves for the free land. Many of them were also seeking refuge to avoid prosecution in their home states for crimes committed there. These gringos made no promises, promoted insurrection, and brought, bought, and sold slaves to others in Texas. By 1836, the Anglos outnumbered the Mexicans in Texas. By 1836, black slaves outnumbered the Mexicans in Texas. Of course, Texas was lost that year, and, within the next fifteen years to 1850, more slaves were brought into Texas to the point that in that year, the census enumeration listed 28 percent of the population as black.

Careful what deal you cut with Anglos. They have a history of broken promises to Mexicans, Native Americans, and blacks.

39. Almost or Already?

The battle of the population figures is ongoing because it is important for the allocation of political power, services, programs, infrastructure development, planning, and the like. Hispanic organizational leaders and other Raza leaders love to quote and cite Anglo demographers that proclaim our numbers were almost 10 percent of the U.S. population in 1990 and would grow to almost 33 million or 12 percent by 2000. Within the Hispanic group, these same organizational leaders and other Raza types loudly proclaim that those of us with Mexican ancestry constitute almost 64 percent of all Hispanics. The truth of the matter is that those of Mexican ancestry are already 65.2 percent of all Hispanics as of March 1999. And we are projected to become 80 percent of all Hispanics by 2050.

Questions: Should we not now get at least 65 percent of all benefits, positions, programs, political power, etc. allocated to Hispanics?
Should we not also demand reciprocity from other Hispanic groups,
namely those with single-digit percentages of population that ride our
demographic coattails?

40. Stone Lost Her Stones

Yes, Sharon Stone, the famous actress, lost her stones (jewelry)
and other items valued at $300,000 to a thief. The caper was pulled at
her Los Angeles home in January 2000. Who does she blame? The
maid, Socorro del Carmen Membreno, who is being held since then
on $300,000 bail for grand theft. Our woman, Socorro, has pled not
guilty to the charges.

Why is it that they always blame the maid? Doesn't home insurance cover theft? Besides, why were Sharon Stone's stones just laying
around inviting someone to lift them? Is there no safe in the home?
How about the bank?

41. English or Español?

Reies López Tijerina wrote his autobiography, *Mi lucha por la
tierra,* many years after the historic exploits that made him a Chicano
hero to my generation. He wrote and had it published in 1978 in Spanish by the renowned Mexican publishing house Fondo de Cultura
Económica. The book was not translated into English until I did it for
Arte Público Press in December 1999.* As a result, few of us have
read the autobiography. Too many of us do not know about the life-
time trials and tribulations that shaped this Chicano hero because we
cannot read in Spanish or even speak the language of our ancestors.
The U.S. educational system makes sure that we cast aside the Spanish we bring from home during the first years of schooling and sub-
stitutes English in its stead.

If you want our people to learn our history, culture, politics, business, ideology, and about our heroines and heroes, write in English.

They Called Me "King Tiger": My Struggle for the Land and Our Rights.

42. Porous Border

The concept of a border, much like a fence, is illusory. It does keep some things out and other things in, but not everything. As you read in the Introduction, crossing the *Gringo Manual* from Mexico to the United States in 1974 should not have been an "illegal act." Importing books was not illegal nor was there a tax to pay for importing books. The U.S. Customs officials at the Eagle Pass, Texas, border, however, deemed it to be "subversive material" and wanted to confiscate the entire print run. I chose to return to Mexico with the books and relied on the traditional routes of commerce utilized by gunrunners, bootleggers, drug smugglers, *coyotes*, and the like, for some of those things police agents cannot keep out or in, to get the books delivered to me in *Cristal.*

There are other things a border or U.S. Customs agents cannot keep out or in—disease, ideas, radio waves, pollution, crime, satellite surveillance, bullets, nuclear missiles, and people.

42. Homey Toys

David Gonzales invented small figurines modeled after male characters in the *barrio* that are an inch or so tall and sell for 50 cents in gumball machines. These figures are dressed in *cholo* garb—baggy pants, hair nets, head bands, some with sunglasses and tattoos, suspenders—and a few are females in short skirts, big hairdos, and heavy make-up. He gave them names like Mr. Raza, Loco, Sapo, Smiley, etc. and calls them Homeys. In 1999 alone he sold more than four million.

His critics came after him. The police and some Hispanic types labeled these figures stereotypical and gangsta-looking. Some Chicanos accused Gonzales of selling our culture for profit because the figurines were being bought by mainstream youth. K-Mart in Dallas, Texas, and some Southern California grocery stores banned them after some press articles came out highlighting the controversy. In other circles, the negative publicity boosted sales. Gonzales then launched a new line, *Mijos,* and has sold two million of these figures.

The success is a result of a powerful demographic—Raza buying power is nearly $400 billion a year. And, Gonzales is only doing what major retailers, such as Foley's, Macy's, Dillard's, J.C. Penney, and Sears, for example, are already capitalizing on. Look at any Sunday newspaper insert, catalog, or daily advertisement for youth clothing: these models have on the baggy pants, long-sleeve shirts, heavy shoes, and other gangsta apparel.

43. Drapes and Zoot Suits

Chicano *pachucos* from El Paso, Texas, started wearing expensive shoes and suits, the zoot suit style, in the late 1930s. They also invented a new slang, *caló*. Both the slang and the dress style were picked up by other *chucos* in Los Angeles and spread from there across the nation. The *chucos* called their outfits "drapes," as well as zoot suits. When Spike Lee immortalized Malcolm X in the movie by the same name, he also created the impression that it was urban blacks, such as Malcolm "Red" Little, in the 1940s who invented the zoot suit style. No! Hollywood makes movies for entertainment without regard to historical accuracy.

44. War Heroes

Telemundo, the Spanish-language television network, developed an epic, two-hour documentary, *Soldados,* on the contribution that Raza soldiers have made in U.S. wars over the centuries, from the Revolutionary War through the Persian Gulf War. In the movie *Saving Private Ryan,* you did not see a single Chicano in the entire film, yet Chicanos were central figures in that war.

Hollywood makes movies for entertainment without regard for appropriate typecasting. And, there are thousands of films made without a single Chicano or Chicana in any role. Usually, they will use colored contact lenses, tanning creams, and hair dye on Anglo actors to make them look Chicano.

45. Rehabilitation

Usually, a person convicted of a crime must not only serve jail time as punishment but also remain on parole after serving the sentence. Sometimes probation is granted as an alternative to serving jail time. Henry Cisneros, the star politician from San Antonio and later Secretary of Housing and Urban Development under President Bill Clinton, was given probation after pleading guilty to a federal misdemeanor. He had lied to the Federal Bureau of Investigation about the extent and amount of money payments he had made to his mistress, Linda Medlar Jones. He then got a job with Univisión, the Spanish-language television network, at a very good salary. And in the first months of 2000, Cisneros began speaking out on behalf of Raza immigrants. The press has begun to report on his policy initiatives, and commentators are suggesting that he is rehabilitating himself. They point to survey research that reveals a favorable image among our Raza. Other politicians mention his name as a potential candidate and acknowledge he is a player once again.

Can a person ever shake the label of having been convicted? Can a person that admitted to lying ever be trusted in high government office? In Henry's case, will his past make him so dependent on the powers-that-be that he becomes a compromised leader?

46. Who Makes Money from Illiteracy?

The U.S.A. spends approximately $225 billion a year in lost productivity due to illiterate persons. According to the American Literacy Council, about 75 percent of unemployed adults have reading or writing difficulties; 60 percent of the prison population are nonreaders; 85 percent of all juveniles offenders have problems reading; nearly $5 billion is spent on unemployment compensation due to illiteracy. Over in the private sector, businesses also spend millions of dollars on low production, workplace accidents, poor product quality, and lawsuits directly related to illiteracy. And, illiterate parents are twice as likely to produce functionally illiterate offspring. Our Raza has, among other terrible indices, a very high illiteracy rate. Why does this problem continue to persist? Could it be that the majority of the illiterates are people of color, like our Raza? Could it be that in our economic system those business losses are part of the cost of doing business? Could it be that an illiterate person is paid less, is easily duped, manipulated, exploited, and intimidated? Could it be that many persons would be out of jobs if illiteracy were wiped out? Recall the War on Poverty programs of the mid-1960s and into the end of the twentieth century? Recall the War on Drugs programs of the mid-1980s and into the end of the twentieth century? Many person and businesses made tons of money fighting those wars, but poverty and drugs have won out!

47. HIV/AIDS

Press reports regularly inform of the growing threat of HIV/AIDS around the world. In early summer 2000, the National Intelligence Council (U.S.) reported* some 33.6 million infected persons in the world. They pinpointed the larger estimates to be located in sub-Saharan Africa, 23.3 million, and another 6 million in South and Southeast Asia. By 2010, Asia and the Pacific could surpass Africa in the numbers of persons with the disease. What about Raza?

Between 1982 and 1992, Raza accounted for 16 percent of all cases reported. And as of 1992, our women accounted for 21 percent of all women diagnosed with AIDS; our men accounted for 16 percent of all cases; and our kids accounted for 25 percent of all AIDS cases! So much for those that tout our majority minority status by the year 2007.

48. To Live or Not to Live, That Is the Question

The right-to-life forces are rabid against abortion. They insist a fetus must have a right to life. Unfortunately, these same forces do not believe a fetus born as baby has a right to a healthy life. In 1990, over one third (38.4 percent) of all Raza children were living in poverty. And Raza children were then only 11 percent of all children in the U.S. Less than half of our children in poverty are covered by public health insurance (Medicaid). Mexican American accounts for 35 percent of all the uninsured. Why?

Between 1980 and 1990, our Raza was the only U.S. racial/ethnic group not to show improvement in socioeconomic status, while other groups at least showed moderate gains. We work, but our jobs do not carry health benefits. We work, but our low wages still keep us in pover-

---

*Check it out at www.cia.gov/cia/publications/nie/report/nie99-17d.html

ty. We work, but legislation, such as the 1994 California Proposition 187 and President Clinton's Welfare Reform, targets our people not to receive federal program assistance if they are not legal residents or citizens.

49. Chocolate: German, Swiss, Hershey's, or Mexican?

"Chocolate is the nectar of the gods" is a quote attributed to the Emperor Moctezuma, found in Spanish chronicles dating to the conquest of Mexico by Hernán Cortez. Yet, most people, Raza included, believe the origin of chocolate to be in Germany or Switzerland, and some even believe that Mr. Hershey from Pennsylvania invented it. Annual per capita consumption of chocolate in the U.S. is 10 to 12 pounds, with 40 percent of females and only 15 percent of males doing the consuming. The difference in gender cravings for chocolate is perhaps explained by the fact that it relieves some premenstrual symptoms. And, no, it does not produce acne.

50. Real Heroes

The U.S. Congress established the Congressional Medal of Honor in 1862 and began presentations to soldiers during the Civil War for valor and heroics. Raza soldiers have received the most Medals of Honor per capita of any ethnic/racial group in the country. In February 2000, some thirty-four years after the fact, another Raza soldier made the ranks: Alfredo Rascón from Oxnard, California, received the medal from President Clinton at the White House. Rascón joined the army at age seventeen and went to Vietnam with the 173rd Airborne Brigade as a medic. Near Song Be River in Long Khanh Province, his squad was pinned down by North Vietnamese machine-gunners. Private Rascón braved machine-gun fire and exploding grenades to rescue his comrades. He took a bullet in the hip that raced up his spine and exited his shoulder blade as he pulled Neil Haffy to safety. As Rascón returned to retrieve Haffy's weapons and ammunition, lest it fall into enemy hands, grenade shrapnel tore his face apart. Several other grenades landed near the squad, and twice Rascón placed his body over those of platoon mates Haffy and Sgt. Ray Compton, to protect them from the blasts. He took the brunt of the explosions. Wounded, deaf, bleeding from ears and nose, Rascón continued to give medical aid to his wounded comrades until a rescue helicopter arrived. Unconscious, Rascón was also airlifted from the battle scene, and the on-board air chaplain issued him last rites. But Pvt. Rascón did not die from his wounds received March 16, 1966. In fact, he was honorably discharged, and a year later he became an American citizen. I forgot to mention that he and his family were from Chihuahua, Mexico. One way to become a U.S. citizen is to join the military. What a price to pay during wartime for citizenship!

In fact, some 60,000 immigrants currently are in the U.S. military forces, and one in five of the Congressional Medal of Honor winners is an immigrant.

51. *Habla español el Bush y también el Gore*

Both presidential candidates in 2000 spoke in Spanish and English to our Raza on the campaign trail. Governor Bush (R-Texas) even proposed a debate *en español*, knowing that Vice-President Gore was just starting to take lessons in Spanish. At the beginning of the election year, February 2000, President Clinton met with Raza leaders three times in one week at the White House. Why? Well, in 1992, Clinton took 61 percent of the Raza vote. In 1996, he took 72 percent of the Raza vote. Now, the polls indicate that Gov. Bush may take 40 percent of the Raza vote. In Texas, Bush, as gubernatorial candidate, received nearly 49 percent of the Raza vote.

The smart Republicans know their candidates cannot win national races without larger than the normal number of votes from Raza for Republicans. Their concern is how to woo Raza Democrats and Independents into the Republican column without promising anything substantive to our group.

The smart Democrats know their candidates cannot win national elections without keeping the Raza voters in the Democratic column, as they have for years. Their concern is how to keep the Raza voting Democrat without promising anything substantive to our group.

52. Rod or Baugh?

The first Raza Republican elected in the past century to the California assembly seat was Rod Pacheco from Riverside. As assemblyman, he had a good salary and six staffers and 655 square feet of office space. Then, he rose up the Republican ranks to become elected Assembly Leader of the Republican Caucus. Now, he was earning $106,425 a year in that job, had a staff of 70, and 2,000 square feet of space. Along came his colleague from Orange County, California, Scott Baugh, who deplored Pacheco's "Hispanic initiatives," such as hiring bilingual staffers, issuing Spanish-language press releases and news *en español* about Republicans. Pacheco was dumped after six months on the job, and Baugh, the new Assembly Leader of the Republican Caucus, also dumped the reforms.

53. "No Mexicans Allowed at Wal-Mart"

In 1994, the state of Mississippi was experiencing a labor shortage. The unemployment rate was about 5 to 6 percent, according to Dorlof "Bo" Robinson, owner of Robinson Farms, a cotton producer for Hamilton Electric Gin and also an elected Public Utility Commissioner for the state. Robinson hired Joe Rojas as a supervisor and asked him to hire more Raza to come work for him and the gin. Rojas hired Mexicans from Harlingen, Texas, to come work the cotton gin. But in September 1994, the men (Robert Treviño, Rudolfo Medrano, Samuel Marfileno, David Mata, Rafael Rosales, Felipe Martínez, Andrés Saavedra, Joel Mendoza, Gilbert Serrato, Juan Aguilar, and Cirilo García) went to buy groceries at the Wal-Mart store in Amory, Mississippi, and were refused the right to shop because they were Mexicans. Security guard David Thompson escorted them out of the store, despite the fact they had shopping carts full of necessary items. The men complained to Rojas, who complained to Robinson. "Bo" couldn't believe the story, so he went to the Wal-Mart store and inquired. Sure enough, David Thompson said he had ordered them out of the store because they were Mexicans. And Thompson ordered them out of the store while Robinson was there making the inquiry. Thompson said he was only carrying out the orders of the store manager not to let Mexicans shop in the store. "Bo" Robinson took them to another store to buy groceries. He does not want his Mexican help to leave the area.

The Raza hired a lawyer, Filemón B. Vela, Jr., from Corpus Christi, Texas, and sued Wal-Mart Stores, Inc. (Civil Action B-94-331). And "Bo" Robinson gave a deposition in the case recounting the story above.

And most Hispanics will tell you they have never been discriminated against, or that the "No Mexicans Allowed" signs disappeared in the 1950s, or that this type of overt racial discrimination only happened to blacks in the deep South. Really?

54. Protected Speech?

As President Ronald Reagan overhauled the Federal Communications Commission's (FCC) rules that had prohibited "hate speech" on the air, mandated equal time, maintained the fairness doctrine, among other policies, all that went out the window. If you want to respond to an attack on radio or television, you have to buy time to do so or sue them for slander. The people of El Cenizo, a city near Laredo, Texas, comprised of nearly 100 percent Mexicans that speak Spanish as their primary language, convinced their city council to conduct council meetings in Spanish. Why speak in English, which only some understood and not in the Spanish that everyone understood? So, the city council voted to conduct council meetings in Spanish. The U.S. crazies involved with the English Only movement and their ilk went bonkers over this "separatist" move. The disk jockeys in Manasas, Virginia, Don Geronimo and Mike O'Meara, of the *Don and Mike Show* on WJFK-FM, called members of the city council in El Cenizo. While on the air, Don and Mike both made derogatory comments to them, insulted them, made fun of them by speaking English with a mocking Spanish accent. "This is America. You Mexicans have your own country." "You Mexicans should get on your burros and go back to Mexico." "Do you have glowing neon underneath your car, on your lowrider?" These were some of the comments made to City Commissioner Flora Barton. She also complained to the FCC of other comments she felt were lewd, obscene, cruel, and hateful.

An Albuquerque, New Mexico, station pulled the *Don and Mike Show* from the airwaves as a result of this incident. Parent corporate owner Infinity Broadcasting Corporation, which aired the show and this program in forty-eight other stations across the country, made Geronimo and O'Meara apologize on the air and by letter to City Commissioner Barton. And when the flap would not die down, ordered a second apology on the air.

Meanwhile, the complaint is on file at the FCC and one of five commissioners there, Gloria Tristani, was appalled at the content of the show. She called the broadcast "one of the most hateful, racist, bigoted, and demeaning pieces of radio that I have heard." But what about the complaint? Commissioner Tristani said, "Now that a complaint has been filed, though, whether or not it also violates the FCC's current rules is another question. And, of course, I will reserve judgment."

Of course.

55. Water, Water Everywhere and Not a Drop to Drink!

Texas alone has more than 1,500 *colonias*, unincorporated areas near a city, that have no basic services, such as water, sewer connections, gas, paved streets, sidewalks, etc. Nearly half a million people, all Raza, live in these *colonias*. Millions more live in the other *colonias* spread across the Southwest.

A provision in the North American Free Trade Agreement (NAFTA), inserted by astute politicos, called for the creation of the North American Development Bank (NAD). The U.S. and Mexico kicked in some money, $25 million, to fund the bank and projects needed in the borderland areas, for example *colonias*. Finally, in late 1999, the Texas Secretary of State, Elton Bomer, proposed to improve living conditions for 30,000 persons along the border near seven cities by providing funding, $8.4 million, from NAD for water and sewer hook-ups. Contractors are out like vultures looking for the jobs.

Isn't it great that by 2002 maybe 5 percent of the half million people in desperate need will be able to drink water, like the rest of us? They will be able to shit, shower, and shave indoors, like the rest of us. And they will be able to complain of how bad their water tastes, like the rest of us.

56. Not at the Bookstore

Many a person turns away disgusted at not finding books on Chicanos at the big bookstore at the mall. If they do find some books, they are few in number and located in some obscure corner and on a high shelf. If you ask why there is no Chicano section with lots of books, the retort by some counter clerk is usually, "Don't know," but they will be glad to order any book you want.

In the fall and winter 1999 catalogs from twenty-five of the nation's most prestigious publishing houses, only 15 of 1,871 titles were by Raza authors. That is less than 1 percent of all books advertised.

The best-known U.S. Chicana author is probably Sandra Cisneros, and her books have crossover appeal. Her publisher is Knopf. Ash Green, senior editor at Knopf, does not believe American publishers shy away from Hispanic authors. "It may just be that, despite the growing Hispanic population, the writing tradition there isn't being developed much."

Can you believe it? We are the ones lacking a writing tradition.

57. How Long Does It Take?

Among lawyers and jurists, the saying "Justice delayed is justice denied" is well quoted in terms of postponed trials and hearings on critical matters affecting a person. Apparently, this adage does not ring true in the halls of the U.S. Senate, which has dragged its feet on judicial nominations made by President Clinton, particularly during his second term in office. Clinton nominated U.S. District Judge Richard A. Paez to the 9th U.S. Circuit Court of Appeals in 1996. The Senate Judiciary Committee is playing games. It does not want to approve Clinton's nominees with George Bush, Jr., waiting in the wings. It matters not to them whether the cases are backlogged in most federal courts. It matters not to them that even Supreme Court Chief Justice William Reinquist has stated his disgust at the slow pace of hearings on nominees.

Judge Paez was finally approved by the Senate on a 59-39 vote on March 9, 2000, the longest wait for any judge in U.S history. There were seventy-three other federal judgeship vacancies pending.

58. Pistol-Packing, Pencil-Pushing *Migra*

Do you know that the Immigration and Naturalization Service (INS) has the dual responsibility of hunting down Mexicans without documents AND processing applications for citizenship? Is this the proverbial fox in the chicken coop? On the hunting-of-Mexicans side of the tasks, the INS has caught more than ever, and its budget has gone up for more agents, faster vehicles, more helicopters and radar, bigger guns, and the like. On the paper processing of applications, the INS has a big problem: backlog. The INS cannot seem to get its act together when it comes to processing paper. Some congressional critics pointed to the outrageously long time it takes the INS from the first receipt of an application to its final approval: twenty-eight months in 1998. In that year, the INS also handled 610,547 cases. In 1999, the INS handled 1.25 million cases and cut the processing time to twelve months. Everybody celebrated, particularly those processed.

The backlog, however, remains. There are more than 1,360,000 persons waiting whose applications still logjammed somewhere in the INS bureaucracy. As some critics point out, maybe it is best for the INS to pick which job it wants to do: hunt or push paper.

59. *Chile Verde, Rojo* or Pepper Spray?

Cambridge, like all cities, holds classes for police cadets on how to become a good police officer. One class taught by Officer Frank Gutoski was about the use of "O.C.," which in police jargon is short for oily resin of capsicum, another name for *chile,* used in pepper spray. In class, Gutoski actually said to the eager-to-learn cadets, "The people that it doesn't affect are people who have consumed cayenne peppers from the time they are small children, and this generally breaks into ethnic categories." The illustrious and informed officer continued to teach that "Mexican Americans tend to be pickers. So, with Cajuns, Mexican Americans, Pakistanis, Indians . . . what happens is the O.C. is effective for a much shorter time."

Fortunately, the city's police commissioner found no empirical or scientific evidence to back Gutoski's claims and soon apologized to the 8 percent of Cambridge's population made up of Raza.

60. The Politics of Scholarships

Almost every Raza organization spends some effort in raising money for scholarships. The scholarships are given to promising Raza children after high school graduation to defray the costs of higher education. Until 1986, no scholarship-giving organization looked into the immigration status of a potential recipient as a criterion. After 1986 and the wave of anti-immigrant legislation introduced and passed in many states, and by the federal government, if the recipient was not a citizen, he or she could not attend any public institution of higher education. Consequently, our children graduating high school who are in the process of adjusting their citizenship status are ineligible to attend a public institution and must apply to a private institution, where the costs of education are prohibitive.

Joshua Ramírez, a graduate of Irving's Nimitz High School in Texas, earned a 4.0 grade point average. His early childhood education was the usual one for a Chicanito entering an English-only environment. He was born in Mexico. His family moved from Mexico to Edinburg, Texas, in 1989. He flunked the second grade because he did not understand English and slowly began to catch on and excel. He also developed an interest beyond academics in the clarinet. He aced the College Board's Hispanic Recognition Program exams. Southern Methodist University (SMU) offered him a partial scholarship of $20,000 for four years. The local community college offered a full scholarship for two years. As a nonresident, Joshua is ineligible for financial aid.

In January 1999, his mom became a legal resident. Now, he might be able to apply for citizenship via his mother. Meanwhile, he wants to go to school at SMU.

Anybody out there have an extra $20,000 a year for Joshua? Yes, it costs about $40,000 a year to attend SMU. Anybody out there know a lawyer who can keep the *migra* from deporting him?

61. Survey Research a la Memphis, Tennessee

Memphis, Tennessee, now has tens of thousands of Raza living in the city. The Memphis Light, Water, & Gas Division of the company wanted to learn more about Raza, so James Overton, an electrical engineer, wrote and distributed a survey questionnaire to "pillars of the community," in order to get their opinion on the Raza. Here are some questions from the thirty he posed: Are Hispanic sometimes squatters? Would you say that Hispanics work three to six months per year and leave without disconnecting the service? Do Hispanics park illegally in handicap [sic] parking spaces? Do Hispanics run up bills and do not wish to pay?

Additionally, the utility company demanded proof of residency or citizenship for someone to receive services. The Washington-based League of United Latin American Citizens (LULAC) took on the fight and made the utility honchos retract the survey, quash the results, and apologize. The utility and LULAC signed a "confidentiality agreement."

Anytime you can't say what the deal is, it means someone got the worst of it. I wonder who.

62. 100 Women of the Century

The Women's Chamber of Commerce of Texas sponsored an event billed as honoring the 100 Women of the Century. A book, *Women of the Century: Inspiring Stories from Great Texas Women,* will be forthcoming. Several Chicanas, eight, made the list: Adina de Zavala, Elizabeth Flores, Jovita Idar, Ninfa Laurenzo, Guadalupe Quintanilla, Irma Rangel, Emma Tenayuca, and Judith Zaffirini.

This number is not bad, 8 of 100; it is less than 10 percent, but more than *nada.*

63. Hate Crimes

Dragging someone chained to the back of a pickup is a heinous crime. Everyone heard of the June 1998, dragging death of James Byrd, Jr., in Jasper, Texas, at the hands of some gringo racists (I know this is redundant), Lawrence Russell Brewer, John William King, and Shawn Allen Berry. The incident made national headlines on radio, television, and newspapers for months until the three were convicted and sentenced.

Meanwhile, back at the other end of Texas, near Sweetwater in West Texas, Tony Chavarría was also beaten, chained to a pickup, and dragged before he freed himself. Like the Jasper killing, he was drinking with some good old boys, and they got to arguing and they beat him, chained him, and dragged him about a mile. He remained in intensive care for days.

Investigators, including the infamous Texas Rangers, said, "Nah, this is not race-related." Only one suspect was charged with aggravated assault.

64. Drug Designation: New Buzz Words

The U.S. Congress has developed a new concept in dealing with the War on Drugs, and is also expanding surveillance capabilities on all kinds of people. The Congress authorizes money and police programs to flow into a geographic area designated as a High-Intensity Drug Trafficking Area. There are seventeen High-Intensity Drug Trafficking Areas already designated across the country. Among them are Atlanta, Chicago, Houston, Los Angeles, Miami, and San Francisco.

Now that North Texas has reached a population of nearly one million Raza, the local U.S. Attorney is asking for the designation for the Dallas-Fort Worth area. He wants money to build a regional investigative support center (intelligence unit), a wiretap center (more intelligence), investigative and prosecutorial task forces (cops, snitches, and prosecutors), drug treatment center (snitch recruiting station), and a drug prevention program (target persons for arrest and prosecution). According to the U.S. Attorney Paul Coggins, "The North Texas High-Intensity Drug Trafficking Area will concentrate on communities with high levels of crime, substance abuse, unemployment, and violence. The fundamental strategy will be to identify criminals and groups who tear down the fabric of the community and target them for arrest and prosecution."

Anybody out there, other than me, read Raza into these words?

65. Migrant or Immigrant?

I read in Webster's dictionary that a migrant was a person that went from one place to another within his or her homeland. I also read that an immigrant was a person that went from one country to another.

If the illegal alien gringos came into Texas and ripped it off by 1836, then the United States invaded Mexico in 1846 and ripped off half of Mexico, and most Mexicans left for the old Mexico to avoid being killed and otherwise oppressed, that means the border came to us. This also means the United States occupied part of Mexico (the Southwest and most of the West) is also our homeland.

So then, are we migrants or immigrants?

66. Surveillance, Now Dataveillance

During J. Edgar Hoover's FBI days, he authorized the collection of information on millions of Americans because he disagreed with their politics. The origin of many counter-intelligence programs (COINTELPROs) can be traced to this era. The role of the FBI agent was to find informants to infiltrate organizations and report to the local FBI Special Agent in Charge (SAC) in the nearest city or the Special Agent operating in the area of their activity. At times, Hoover would authorize a COINTELPRO be directed at persons or organizations to destroy them. The specific destructive tactics varied but included wiretaps, purloined letters, disinformation, rumor mongering, promoting and inciting illegal activity, physical surveillance, break-ins into offices for theft of files, and the like.

Today, this activity continues but is augmented by technology. Every time you use a credit card to make a purchase, you provide information on your whereabouts, time and place, goods or services bought, amounts, and credit limits. Look at your monthly statement and see if you cannot reconstruct your whereabouts and activities from that itemized list of purchases. Every time you make a phone call, particularly on a cell phone, or you use a pager, you also establish your whereabouts, time and place, numbers called, and if a government agency has a wiretap, even the content of the conversation. If you call from a car phone or use the equipment in a car, you are also establishing your whereabouts and the general direction headed. Some people are even buying software that beams location to a satellite to alert others of their whereabouts in case of an emergency. Every time you enter a secured building or use a machine that has a security code to grant or deny access, send e-mail on the Internet, or buy a product through the computer, you are leaving an electronic trail. This is dataveillance, and it is now the main source of information on people.

Have a wonderful time with your cell phone, e-mail, credit card, pager, beeper, and other codes.

67. Scabs, Strikebreakers, Now Union Recruits

In the early 1970s, I initiated dialogue with the government of Mexico, namely with President Luis Echeverría Álvarez, while I was the national president of the Raza Unida Party. I sought out other Chicano leaders to join me in that dialogue. All resisted my invitations, except for Reies López Tijerina, for many years—especially César Chávez. He believed that Mexican nationals were the strikebreakers in many of his battles with growers and thought of them as the enemy. Organized labor did also. In many conversations, Chávez would oppose my proposals to participate in the binational debate (U.S.-Mexico) on immigration to allow more Mexicans to cross. Later in his career, Chávez changed his mind and did meet with Mexican officials and union leaders to discuss collaboration on recruitment of workers, strikes, and the Mexican government's social security program. Organized labor remained steadfast in opposition to the presence of Mexican labor, and especially to recruitment into labor's ranks in the United States.

Lo and behold, with the rise of union leaders such as Jaime Martínez in the International Union of Electrical Workers and Linda Chávez-Thompson, an AFL-CIO executive vice-president, among others, organized labor has made an about-face. On June 3, 2000, the national leadership of organized labor called for new laws to criminalize employer exploitation of undocumented workers, grant amnesty, and extend permanent residency to immigrants working here illegally.

I guess the unions now care more about union cards than green cards. Besides, who else is there to organize?

68. Nashville *norteño*

Nashville, Tennessee, conjures up images and sounds of country music. Not anymore! In Murfreesboro and Nashville there are three independently owned, 5,000-watt AM stations (WMGC, WNQM, WHEW) playing Mexican music for the area's 30,000 immigrants; one in thirteen persons in the Nashville area is Mexican.

Nationwide, the trend is the same with Mexican stations taking the lead in Arbitron ratings in places like Los Angeles, where KSCA-FM and KLVE-FM hold the number one and two spots in the entire radio market, respectively. In New York, radio station WSKQ-FM holds the number three slot, and in Miami, radio station WAMR-FM holds the number four spot. In Dallas, Chicago, San Francisco, Albuquerque, Denver, Houston, and other major cities, radios are blasting *salsa, norteño, regional, tejano, cumbias, conjunto,* and *merengues.* This music format now played in more than 500 stations across the United States generated in excess of $440 million dollars in advertising revenue in 1998, and it is growing.

This is the good news. The bad news is Raza does not own the overwhelming number of these stations. As usual, we are making money for others.

69. "Whatever You People Want to Call Yourselves"

Surely you have heard a speaker addressing a Raza crowd say something similar to the title to this trick. And surely you have been at a meeting when someone who wants to delay, disrupt, obstruct, or otherwise bring chaos into the equation proposes a name change of the organization from Chicano to Latino, Hispanic, etc. This occurred on a mass scale in the early 1980s across campuses, communities, and regions. The truth of the matter is that we as a people are not in charge of the group label in English; the U.S. Bureau of the Census is. Before 1940, we were classified as Other Race; Caucasian (they baptized us as white); in the 1950s we were Latin Americans; in the 1960s we were Mexican American; in the 1970s we were Americans of Spanish Surname; and since the 1980s, we have become Hispanics. Asked in Spanish, any one of us will respond with Mexicano or Chicano or Raza, and the cultural cousins from Puerto Rico, Cuba, Panama, Honduras, Guatemala, El Salvador, and other such countries will say their nationality—*soy nicaragüense,* for example.

We are not in charge of group identification nor in control of the labeling. We are only in charge of the in-fighting with one another over the labels. That is the purpose—intragroup division over ethnicity and intergroup division over race.

71. I'm Chicana. I'm Latina. I'm Hispanic.

"What does Chicano mean?" "Where did it come from?" "Does it mean low-life Mexican?" You have heard that before. Rudolfo Acuña, author of *Occupied America,* titled a more recent book *Anything But Mexican.* He hit the nail on the head. Most of us run away from our Mexicanness. We would rather be anything but Mexican. So, the current trend is to be Hispanic or try to be less "Spanish" and claim to be Latino. Well, Hispanic does come from a Spanish origin, but Latino comes from Napoleon III. When he attempted to enter and establish a foothold in the Americas, he proclaimed it as Latin America and its people "Latinos", closer to France than Spain in language, heritage, and tradition.

What is the difference is claiming to be Latino or Hispanic? Only choosing one European power over another as the ancestral origin.

72. I'm white. I'm Indian. I'm *Mestizo.*

We fight each other over the proper racial identity also. History tells us that the Moors (African followers of Muhammad's Islam) invaded Spain in 711 and occupied the land until 1491. That is 780 years! During that time do you think the Moors were celibate? Cristoforo Colombo and his crew were discovered in 1492 by the Taínos and Caribs off their coast near present-day Haiti and the Dominican Republic. Only Spanish men (there were some Catholic priests and African slaves among the "conquistadores") continued to arrive in the New World for the next 127 years! During this century and a quarter, do you think the Spaniards and priests and slaves were celibate? Mexico endured invasions by gringos from 1820 to 1836 and again from 1846 to 1848; from the French from 1859 to 1862; and the dictator Porfirio Díaz invited scores of European immigrants to settle in Mexico during his reign until 1910. Do you think these invaders and immigrants were celibate?

I think that rather than argue over racial identity and purity, Raza ought to learn from Anglos. Haven't you noticed that almost every Anglo will claim to be part Cherokee?

73. *La Cookie*

When I was a kid, *la cookie* meant an Oreo or a chocolate-chip cookie or a fig newton. As an adolescent, I learned it had sexual meaning for a female body part. Now, *la cookie* is a menace to your computer. A cookie is a small data file sent by a Website and written to your hard disk. The good news: Every time you visit the sending Website, it identifies you and grants you access quicker. The bad news: Once in place, it tracks everything you do both on the sending site's Web page and wherever else you go on the Web!

Find out how to get those cookies out of your hard disk. There is hell to pay with some companies. Hotmail, Yahoo, Amazon.com, and the *New York Times,* for example, will stop you cold online unless you allow them to identity confirmation at almost every link. There are many others.

74. *El* Spam

Like the cookie in Trick Number 73, there is also Spam. No, it is not what you used to eat as a kid or while in college for dinner. Spam in this day and computer age is junk mail. There are two kinds: e-mails you request, like the bargains on airfare and the porno sites you click on and have hell trying to get out of. Every time you answer a questionnaire online, reveal data for survey research, or enter a contest for a prize, you've set yourself up for Spam! Don't use your main e-mail address! Use another address that will get all the junk stuff, especially for chat rooms. Unsubscribe to the junk you don't want to keep receiving.

75. New Taxes and User Fees

The U.S. Postal Service used to be a real service in that it did not have to turn a profit because it was a government agency funded by our tax dollars. Guess what? They are now the biggest proponent of a user fee for e-mail. They propose a fee of ten cents per e-mail. Their argument is that they are losing millions on people not using stamps to mail their messages.

I thought taxpayer dollars already had funded the research and development that led to the Internet. I thought that while the actual transmission of the e-mail is free, the services to log on and the equipment to access the Internet are not. Raza cannot afford the equipment and service as it is, much less the user fee per e-mail. A better proposal would be to charge the television and radio companies a huge user fee for our air space through which they send out their signals to households and make tons of money.

76. White Man's Burden

While doing research at the Zimmerman Library at the University of New Mexico in Albuquerque, I noticed three good-sized murals on a wall facing the staircase I used daily to gain access to my office. The murals depict laborers, Mexican and Native Americans, in various action positions. In each mural there is a white, male person, child or full-grown man, amidst these laborers. The white male has eyes and the laborers do not. In one mural, the white dude has the laborers by the hand, leading them somewhere. Ah, what terrible burden white men have to carry, leading us, seeing for us, guiding us, and being the ones who can really see things as they are.

The murals have been regularly defaced by some person(s), adding eyes to the laborers only to have the paintings restored. Why are they not taken down?

77. "I'm Sorry"

Gringos love to say the phrase "I'm sorry" for everything and on any occasion, especially when they have committed a serious transgression against you. "I'm sorry" is better salve than *sávila,* aloe vera, in their culture. Gringos say this phrase so much, so often, it is meaningless, and therefore more offensive. The gringo does not learn the Chicano way. You screw up by offending someone (Raza that understands the culture) and you better run, duck, hide, move far away, or crawl into a hole because that someone will come looking for you. "I'm sorry" will just not cut it!

The correct Raza etiquette in a case of a transgression is to say both "I'm sorry" and then, quickly add, "Will you forgive me?" The last part gives the victim or offended person the right to accept or reject the apology for the transgression.

78. Taco or Tatcho

One of the finest Chicano Studies programs in the nation is found at the University of Houston under the direction of Dr. Tatcho Mindiola, a sociologist. Dr. Mindiola got this program funded in a big way several years ago by personally going to the Texas legislature and lobbying for money for his program because the university did not think it was a priority. Over the years, Dr. Mindiola made many friends in the legislature and regularly invited them over to the campus. On one occasion, the Mexican American Legislative Caucus held a meeting at the main campus, and Dr. Mindiola placed the university president on the agenda to give welcoming remarks to the legislative delegation. The president was very pleased that Dr. Mindiola had included him because he would have a chance to impress the legislators with all the good the university was doing and all the extra money it needed to keep it up. The president welcomed the legislators and Dr. Mindiola profusely and repeatedly.

The problem was, he called him Taco, not Tatcho, several times, even after he was shouted at by the legislators with the correct name. Tatcho finally had to rescue him by telling him near his face, "My name is Tatcho, not Taco."

79. "I Want to Run"

A Salvadoran friend of Chicanos in the Dallas area decided he, too, wanted to run for office. "Why just Chicanos?" he asked on several occasions at meetings of the Mexican American Democrats (MAD) of the Texas chapter in Dallas. Not many Salvadorans or Central Americans, for that matter, are eligible to run for public office because, like many Mexicans, they are not citizens. Central Americans are here on temporary visas, mostly. But not Marcial Trejo; he was a citizen and active in the communities, both Chicano and Salvadoran. MAD screened him and endorsed his candidacy. Mr. Trejo eagerly went with cash in hand for the filing fee on the last day of the period to file as candidate for the office of Justice of the Peace in Precinct 8 for Dallas County, Texas, and was rejected.

The Election Code rules in place in 1998 required a filling fee *and* valid signatures of eligible voters supporting your nomination. He forgot to check the rules. He also forgot to give himself enough time to correct any defect with his paperwork. Forget the stealth campaign approach. Do it right and do it early.

80. Take It to a Higher Level?

Dan Morales was a product of Affirmative Action, like Clarence Thomas, the black face on the U.S. Supreme Court. Dan Morales attended Harvard University, got a law degree, and returned home to San Antonio's West Side and was elected to the state legislature. Soon, he ran and won the office of attorney general for the entire state of Texas, the first Chicano to accomplish this electoral feat. He was hailed as the best thing since Henry Cisneros by some gringos, most Anglos, and many Raza. Then came Cheryl Hopwood and others and filed a lawsuit against the University of Texas Law School for discriminating against white applicants. They blamed their denial of admission on the Affirmative Action (AA) policy in place that allowed minorities to gain admission. The case ultimately went up to the U.S. 5th Circuit Court of Appeals, which entered a ruling declaring the UT-Law School AA program unconstitutional because it used race as a criterion in violation of the Fourteenth Amendment. Rather than watch what UT-Law School would do or if he really felt compelled by some extraterrestrial force to step in and urge compliance with the new case law, what did Attorney General Dan Morales do? He issued an opinion that *all* Texas public institutions of higher learning had to do away with AA.

The gringos all loved him, many Anglos loved him, most Raza and blacks now hate him. Is this what people mean when they say they are taking it to a higher level?

81. Fiesta Time. Party Time.

Back when, the Raza organization in charge of the *fiestas patrias*, for example, or other culturally relevant festivities usually was the local *mutualista*. During the Chicano Movement when we reconnected with our Mexicanness and the notion of a homeland, Aztlán, the Raza sponsored new *fiestas*, such as *Cinco de Mayo,* which is not as celebrated in Mexico as it is in the U.S., and Hispanic Heritage Month. Now, you cannot go to a *fiesta*, cultural or otherwise, that is not heavily sponsored by corporations. The beer signs, cigarette signs, soft drink signs, are everywhere. The credit card people are there asking for you to fill out an application and they hand you goodies . . .

The *fiesta* has become an excuse for a party, just another drinking binge. But they build product loyalty while they use our culture as a commodity.

82. Taxes and More Taxes: Bond Issues

We live in neglected areas of the community because we are not a priority for the elected officials in charge of budget and policy. Budget allocation and spending are merely a reflection of what Anglos value as important to them. When these policymakers need extra cash to spend on a favorite project, they propose a bond election. This is a voter referendum on accepting additional taxes for these projects. The elected officials come out in mass to cheer the Raza to vote FOR the bond issue on the ballot. Usually, some smart Raza group will demand a swimming pool, a cultural center, a street paved, a park, a clinic, a library, etc. in the Chicano part of town as exchange for a vote FOR the bond issue. The elected officials are eager to please and add ONE item for Raza to ALL THEIR OTHER items on the ballot.

The bond issue passes and the Raza get to pay more taxes for a generation or two and receive little or no services or benefits from the other items on the ballot. Over the years as the bond issue matures, the Raza get to watch scores of bond counsel attorneys, underwriters, brokerage houses, financial advisors, and bankers (all overwhelmingly white) make huge fees for putting the deal together. ¡*Qué* nice! The Raza got the swimming pool or the cultural center, etc., maybe even a user fee attached to enjoy the pool.

83. Taxes and More Taxes: Appraised Value

Amado Peña made Chicano art famous. He is the one that paints those Indian-looking figures with one eye looking at you or one slit for an eye not looking at you, surrounded by beautiful colors of mountains and scenery. Every furniture store you go to has these hanging on the walls, and every Chicano from the *movimiento* days may even still have a numbered print from Amado on his household wall. He settled down and opened an art gallery in Santa Fe, New Mexico, along with a couple of thousand other artists. Santa Fe is the oldest capitol in the nation. Our ancestors, Native and Spanish, built the place. Santa Fe has become *the* trendy place to live. Gringos and Anglos from all over have moved to the new mecca: Santa Fe. New homes have been built, old homes bought, especially the real adobe ones owned by Raza. Property has been reappraised and values of homes and have shot up.

Raza cannot afford to live in Santa Fe anymore. The trailer courts on the outskirts of town are where Raza live. They commute to work in Santa Fe. And guess who can vote in elections now? Those that live in the city or those that live outside the city?

84. *La Virgen de Guadalupe* or *La Lupe?*

Back in the days of the Chicano Movement in Texas, there was a youth organization called MAYO (Mexican American Youth Organization).* Irma Mireles from San Antonio became a member, leader, and official in that local chapter. Then she moved to Juneau, Alaska, and began work there among the Raza. She helped expand a radio program and defended the rights of immigrants before government agencies and testified at legislative hearings on many subjects of interest to the Raza.

Soon she approached the Catholic Church about mass *en español*. But the church had no such mass, nor did they have a statue or mural of *La Virgen de Guadalupe*. Irma had heard from Raza old-timers (Yes, we have been in Alaska a long time also!) that they recalled a

---

*See also Armando Navarro's book, Mexican American Youth Organization: Avant-Garde of the Chicano Movement in Texas. Austin: University of Texas, 1995.

painting of her that had once hung on a main wall in the church. Irma asked for it and was told it did not exist. Undaunted, Irma got permission to look in the church basement and found *La Lupe* trashed and dumped in a corner.

Irma pulled her out, cleaned her up, and literally, with the help of others, hung *La Virgen de Guadalupe* on a main wall once again. The Raza got word, and thousands came to worship and attend mass, even if it was in English. Symbols are powerful.

85. Chicano FBI?

Is this an oxymoron? No, in fact, Chicano FBI agents sued the FBI because of job discrimination and won. There are now hundreds of Chicanos and Chicanas in the FBI and other government police agencies, particularly the border patrol. Look around, these folks want to be cops and hunt us.

The Chicano FBI agents also do undercover work because they look like Raza. For decades now, the FBI, CIA, DEA, NSA, IRS, SS, and many other government police agencies have intelligence gathering arms, and they target political activists and organizations. They seek to destroy the leaders and the organizations. Tim Chapa was an undercover agent in New Mexico who targeted the Raza Unida Party members, Reies López Tijerina, Students For a Democratic Society, among others. He helped set up the murder of two Black Berets: Rito Canales and Antonio Córdova. He tried to frame David Tijerina, the oldest son of Reies López Tijerina. He knew that Reies López Tijerina's wife, Patsy, was going to be raped by a state police officer. He did this because it was his job and got paid for it. How do I know this?

I interviewed him on videotape, and when I write the book on federal surveillance of the Chicano Movement and its leaders, you can learn more. Meanwhile, be careful of what you ask for, you just might get it.

86. Border Coverage Program

If we go by turf, the FBI is supposed to be vigilant of crime within the United States. The CIA is supposed to be vigilant of threats to the national security from outside the United States. Well, in the late 1960s the FBI decided it had to go not only outside the U.S. and into CIA territory, but also do its nasty job of political surveillance and counter-intelligence (COINTELPRO). The FBI went to Mexico. This COINTELPRO was called BOCOV for Border Coverage Program.

All along the U.S.-Mexico border, the FBI had agents and informants disrupting organizations and leaders on both sides of the border well into the 1980s. The targets on the U.S. side were exercising their First Amendment rights of free speech, association, assembly, and redress of grievances. The targets on the Mexican side were none of the FBI's business. How did it get away with it?

Mexico didn't say anything. The FBI does what it wants to. When the U.S. Congress held hearings on domestic surveillance abuse by the FBI, the members of Congress did not ask about this extralegal, extraterritorial FBI operation. And the FBI did not and has not admitted to conducting this COINTELPRO.

I know about it because I asked for the documents under the Freedom of Information Act.

87. $10,000 Bounty

A Mexican national, Carlos Ibarra Pérez, age sixty, held a press conference on the steps of city hall in Reynosa, Tamaulipas, Mexico. He announced a bounty of $10,000 to anyone who would kill a U.S. Border Patrol agent. Pérez, like many Mexicans and those who support them, are angry at the callousness and indifference with which U.S. and Mexican authorities accept U.S. Border Patrol brutality and abuse of persons crossing the Rio Grande into their other homeland. And now, even vigilantes in Arizona are calling hunting parties together to go hunt Mexicans near Douglas, Arizona.

All hell broke loose for Pérez, and he was immediately set under investigation and harassment by both U.S. and Mexican officials. He now says he regrets saying such a thing, that he was quoted out of context. It was a dumb thing to say, and also criminal. But it is okay for those with guns and badges or vigilante gringos in Arizona to do so.

88. Can't Swim, *Señor?*

In early June 2000, a videotape was made by a Televisa film crew near Matamoros, Tamaulipas, Mexico, of U.S. Border Patrol agents blocking the path to the Rio Grande of three Mexican nationals attempting to cross the river into the United States. It was broadcast live on both U.S. and Mexican television stations. Why the interest? Well, one of the three men not allowed to get to shore on the U.S. side was able to swim back into the Mexican side of the river. The other two men, Walter María Sandoval of San Lucas, Michoacán, Mexico, and the other unidentified man, either were too tired to swim back or were overpowered by the river currents or could not swim at all. They drowned live on videotape with the border patrol watching.

89. Not in Texas

Texas Governor George W. Bush, Jr., often stated publicly that the California Propositions, such as 187 (no health, no education for undocumented persons), 209 (no Affirmative Action), 227 (no bilingual education), and 21 (try juveniles as adults) would never happen in Texas. Many Raza voters love George "Dubya" [now U.S. President] because of this type of statement. I wish I had these dumb Raza voters in my basic and introductory political science classes. California has the initiative and referendum method for citizens to put ballot measure to vote. Texas does not. Duh! It cannot happen in Texas; it is against the state constitution.

90. Belated Christmas Present: December 29, 2000

On December 29, 2000, the U.S. General Accounting Office (GAO) delivered a report to both House and Senate Appropriations Committees on Guadalupe-Hidalgo land grant claims in New Mexico. The measure was sponsored by the two New Mexican senators, Jeff Bingaman (Democrat) and Pete Domenici (Republican). The bill called for the Department of Justice to investigate the claims. House-Senate conferees gutted that provision and substituted the GAO, and the sponsors felt this was better than nothing, and it was passed by both chambers on October 18, 1999.

The crucial reason for substituting the Department of Justice with the GAO is that a Department of Justice study would have full legal standing and the GAO study would not. In other words, the GAO will be another report saying the land was stolen. A Justice Department study would lead to civil and perhaps criminal charges against those who have stolen the land and have conspired with those who stole the land.

91. What Was the Deal?

Surely you've heard about the Mexican railroad killer? It was sensational news for weeks across the nation. He was on the FBI's Most Wanted List. Finally, a Texas Ranger tracked down Ángel Maturino Reséndiz and the killer's sister. He cut a deal for Marturino Reséndiz's surrender. It is alleged by the family that they agreed to surrender him if he would not get the death penalty. The Texas Ranger says he made no such deal. Yet, Ángel just walked across the bridge into the U.S. and into the handcuffs of the heroic *rinche.* And on May 20, 2000, he was sentenced to death.

If that was not the deal, why would the family urge him to surrender? If he was safe (at least for the time) in Mexico, why come across and give yourself up and stand trial, knowing Texas has the death penalty and an eager governor that routinely denies clemency or delays executions of minorities? The governor has staved off two white killers from death recently.

92. Your Social Security Number

When the Social Security Act was passed into law in 1936, the number was not to be used as an identification number, certainly not by the government. In 1974, with passage of the Privacy Act, providing your social security number to a government agency can either be voluntary or mandatory. You don't decide which option is which, the government does. Under current law, you must disclose the number (not actually have the card!) for child support enforcement, food stamps, IRS, Medicaid, Medicare, Social Security, of course, public assistance, state tax units, Supplemental Security Income, Temporary Assistance for Needy Families *and* state motor vehicle departments. In other words, to get a driver's license, you must produce a social security number. But don't try that, bring the card! You will not get a driver's license or get a renewal without the actual card.

Do you know that only persons who are citizens or legal residents have social security (SS) cards? Therefore, noncitizens and nonresidents can only get a driver's license with a fake SS number or card. What does citizenship have to do with driving? Do you care if the person driving toward you or behind you is a citizen, or do you care if he passed the actual technical requirements for a driver's license?

93. "¡Qué ovarios y huevos!"

Most undocumented persons run for cover when they spot a possible police agent of any sort, and spend their lives living clandestinely. Not anymore! In Los Angeles, Dallas, and Chicago, to name a few major, major metropolitian areas, undocumented persons from Mexico, protested publicly their working conditions and pay scales. They were janitors doing maintenance in downtown buildings. Somebody has to do it! They were ignored by the *coyote* subcontractors, their union leaders, and the corporate bosses of the buildings. They went on strike! In Chicago, some 4,500 of them were on strike for ten days— in Los Angeles and Dallas, thousands more. They won major concessions in all cities and ratified new contracts in April 2000! *¡Sí se puede!*

94. Binationalism

Have you heard of assimilation, integration, and cultural separatism? If so, you are either a bright student that reads or a *veterano* from the Chicano Movement days when the discussion of ideology always batted these terms around. How about binationalism?

It is a new term coming into vogue, now that in many geographic spaces across the U.S. there are more Mexican nationals than Chicano people. These Mexican nationals are frankly perplexed at the Chicano notion of Aztlán, particularly as a political goal. They want to know why we only want half of it and not all of it, *¿Un México?* Good question.

Regardless of what Chicano people say or do, the Mexican nationals, right now, are busy defining what it means to be a resident of two nations, a citizen in two nations, a binational being. They met en masse in Dallas, Texas, and formed a national coalition to impact both Mexican and U.S. policy. You go, *vatos!*

95. No Pass, No Play

The focus in education recently had to do with the practice of passing athletes in courses so they would be in good academic standing and continue to play. Now, most states have some version of the rule that if you do not pass, you do not play, and the academic performance is monitored. Now there is another focus, and that is on the performance of athletes during a game. Two Chicano kids, one in San Antonio and another in Houston during the 1999–2000 academic year, have been charged with criminal assault for hitting another player during a game. Isn't this what contact sports like basketball, football, and soccer are all about?

No gringo kid has been charged, only Raza. Both Chicanos have gotten fined and jail sentences. The student in San Antonio received five years in the penitentiary for breaking another kid's nose.

96. *El mero Gallo*

During the 1960s, 70s, 80s and 90s, Raza protested and often boycotted Gallo wine for unfair labor practices involving the United Farmworkers Union of America (Chávez's UFW). Along came San Antonio artist Joe Luis López and developed a logo in 1997 with a rooster on it and labeled it *"Puro Gallo."* The giant winemaker Ernest & Julio Gallo Winery found out about this "infringement" on their trademark and sued López. And López lost!

If you think this was not only an infringement on Lopez's right to use a rooster and the words *"Puro Gallo,"* but also an appropriation of our cultural symbols . . . *el mero gallo* . . . express yourself: Gallo Winery, P.O. Box 1130, Modesto, California, 95353.

97. The Brown/Black Binary

Raza and blacks have no history of relations until the mid-1940s because of the military and movement into the cities. Sometimes the relationship is good, sometimes it is real bad. President Clinton, as does the entire nation, thinks only in terms of blacks and whites. When he ordered a National Dialogue on Race and formed a commission, he only included blacks and whites, then was made to reorganize and add one Raza member. He did the same dance with the Immigration Reform Commission, one Raza, *y era el más republicano de todos, Richard Estrada, en paz descanse.*

When Clinton tried to bring his Race Commission panel of eleven members on Sports and Race to Houston (taped by ESPN) on April 14, 1998, he was met by angry Chicanos because the panel was AGAIN all black and white, no Raza! Texas State Senator Mario Gallegos took to the streets to protest. Well-known political consultant Marc Campos took to the airwaves and met personally with Clinton staffers to protest. LULAC leader and community activist Johnny Mata issued press releases and also took to the streets, threatening to shut down the event before it happened. Clinton listened and responded. He invited Felipe López to sit on the panel.

The Raza was shut up, but López, a black Hispanic and basketball player from St. John's University, was from the Caribbean.

98. Beat the Student or the Principal?

When I went to school, the principal had a paddle and beat students. In February 1999, Norman Berstein was beaten by two men outside his school building. He told police one of the men that assaulted him was a Hispanic. Berstein was the principal of Burton Street Elementary in Panorama City in the San Fernando Valley of California. The school has 750 students, 90 percent Raza. The parents complained for several years of Berstein's hostile attitude toward them, his opposition to bilingual education, and his permitting one day to celebrate *el cinco de mayo* while making the Razita enjoy a month of Black History and eight other months of Anglo curriculum.

The school authorities in this school, and in Inglewood High School in another part of the city, have dropped both Black History month and *cinco de mayo* for fear of violence and student walkouts. In May 1998, Inglewood had to close for a day after a student rebellion broke out over the very same thing: one day for Raza, one month for blacks, and eight months for whites. Yet, the Raza are the overwhelming numbers of students.

99. Cash or Insurance?

A recent study in Corpus Christi, Texas, found that Raza are more prone to having a stroke than whites, up to three times the rate. If true, this means serious bodily injury with permanent damage or even death. The real killer is not the diet or the body shape or bad genes. The real killer is the lack of money and/or medical insurance.

According to the study done, when you show up in an emergency room with symptoms of a stroke, if you have cash on hand or medical insurance, the ER personnel will administer a CAT scan to determine what is wrong. If you do not have the money or the insurance, they don't do the CAT scan and you can die.

I'm sorry.

100. The Chicano Manual on How to Handle Gringos

As a group, Raza has begun to reach critical mass in terms of voters in certain areas. In turn, this voting bloc is now electing significant numbers of Raza to public office and to very powerful positions in local and state government. In state legislatures, for example, New Mexico has 41 Raza legislators out of 112; that is 36.61 percent. California has 24 Raza legislators out of 120; that is 20 percent. Texas has 35 Raza legislators out of 181; that is 19.34 percent. Arizona has 11 Raza legislators out of 90; that is 12.22 percent. New Mexico and California not only have impressive numbers in the legislature, but many of them are in leadership roles. Manny Aragón is the Senate president pro tempore in New Mexico, along with seven other statewide leaders. In California, the lieutenant governor is Cruz Bustamante and speaker of the assembly is Antonio Villarigosa, and three others have important leadership roles. More than 5,000 elected officials in local government are Raza. While we have a sizable delegation of Raza in Congress, they are still too few and too new, and some are right-wing Cubans. We still do not have a U.S. senator. We are growing in political power.

It is time to write the *Chicano Manual on How to Handle Gringos* because behind each victory of each person mentioned above is a story of how he turned the tables on the gringo and won. Watch for it soon.

PART III

A Gringo Manual on
How to Handle Mexicans

by José Angel Gutiérrez

First published in 1974

Dedication

To the next Chicano generation of Adrián and Tozi.

Acknowledgments

This book would not have been possible without the assistance and labor of: Luz Gutiérrez, María Hernández, Carlos Guerra, Gene Monroe, Janie Monroe, John Fry, José Torres, Laurencio Peña, Elisena Mata, Gloria Ramírez, Joe Rubio, Henry Barker.

Contents

---

[1]For the culturally deprived, *pilón*—a little *lagniappe*[2] thrown in for good measure.
[2]For the culturally deprived, *lagniappe* (lan-yapp) among the Cajuns of Louisiana means *pilón,* a little something extra.

Preface

This little book is intended for Chicanos only, but I am sure it will fall into the clutches of the enemy from time to time. They will certainly profit from it. However, Chicanos should profit even more.

These pages do not exhaust the subject of all the devious, treacherous, hypocritical gringo machinations used against our Raza. But there is a good collection here. Chicanos who know the gringo tricks[3] won't be fooled by them anymore. That's why we are in control of Cristal.[4]

All of my experience has taught me that situations repeat themselves; tactics are predictable. Winners know about situations and tactics. Losers don't. It's as simple as that.

My travels have taken me to every state west of and most of the states east of the Mississippi. To this day, I marvel at the universality of the tactics employed by the haves against the have-nots. These tactics, or better yet, these *tricks* render the opposition virtually impotent. The have-nots have not taken the time to study the situations and to categorize the tricks employed against them. Time and again while speaking at a rally, university, conference, or party, I am asked umpteen questions on tactics, strategy, and organization. Basically, there are two types of questions: the tortilla question and the taco question.

Naïve listeners who want to show their efforts generally ask tortilla questions. One of them might say, "I've called many meetings to

---

[3]Trick—*Movida.* Chicanos know that *movida* means at least six things: 1. A maneuver in business, 2. A mistress or "other woman," 3. A trick, 4. A move, as in chess, 5. A move from one place to another, 6. A bad turn of events, "movida chueca."

[4]Cristal—Crystal City, Texas, a Chicano community that in 1969 boycotted the school. The result has been the total electoral victory of the city, school, and county through the Raza Unida Party.

organize a protest against so and so and nobody came. How do you get people to a meeting?" He is baffled that the people have not responded. This is a typical tortilla question. It can be recognized by its content: It is elitist in nature: you don't make people come to a meeting; you take meetings to the people. You don't impose an issue on the community; the community raises the issue. Organizing really mobilizes what is already there. People should be presented with the problem and the solution. A good organizer knows the solutions before he tackles the problems. The making of tortillas, as all good Chicanos know, requires years of practice. You can't learn how to make tortillas by asking questions. Recent converts to the Chicano Movement, like gringos, want to learn tortilla making from a cookbook recipe. Impossible!

A taco question is posed by an eager learner who asks, "How-do-you-do-X?" He needs to learn something important. He seeks information to "explain" a previous situation he has experienced. He wants to avoid a similar situation because in the previous situation something went wrong and he lost. This is a taco question. Making tacos is a delicate matter. You have to put the meat first, lettuce,[5] tomatoes, then the chile. Taco questions seek to learn the basic underpinnings of the social problem, the ingredients that make the issue complex, and what to do with it. For example, "How do you organize a school boycott?" is a taco question. This type of question demands a full and practical answer. The person who asks such a question wants to know so that he can do. Taco questions and not tortilla questions are obviously the concern of this book.

There are nine categories of tricks. The Law and Order and Demonstrations categories are practically self-explanatory. They deal with the tactics of civil disobedience. Tricks on Education cover the politics of discrimination, as well as the techniques employed to push out our people. Foundation and Political categories are very similar. They are both public structures. Both of them say one thing and do another. A large part of this trick category lists the ways these institu-

---

[5]Union lettuce, of course.

tions shrug off their responsibility. Job tricks deal with employment problems Chicanos regularly run into.

The seventh trick category deals with the information media and their ways of presenting dishonest news as fair and objective reporting. The eighth category covers the pitfalls of negotiations not built into the negotiation process but dug by the opposition. A ninth and final category is a miscellaneous catch-all category.

I present this beginning list of tricks with one end in view. I want Chicanos to employ this knowledge systematically against the gringo.

Granted, the years of oppression will not be ended with this book—or any book. I realize that books in themselves do not end oppression. In line with that realization I have omitted discussion of ideology and philosophy. My purpose is not to describe the philosophical underpinnings of the U.S. of A. This book is a limited manual on how to deal with a racist, imperialist, colonialized society of white people.

Chicanos cannot live by theory alone; we must pick up tools of our liberation. This book is a tool.

Foundation Category

Trick Number 1: Throw Out the Bone

That Chicanos have a difficult time sticking together is a well-known gringo stereotype. A standard South Texas joke tells about the fisherman who walks away from a freshly caught basket of crabs. A passerby yells to him that his catch will soon slither away. "Don't worry," the fisherman replies. "They're Mexican crabs. They'll pull each other down."

In 1970, the Hogg Foundation of Texas announced the availability of funds for a Chicano mental health project. Groups of Chicanos from throughout the state met for the purpose of soliciting the money. The Foundation people threw out the bone. "Whichever group the people assembled here can agree on will get the funds," they said. They expected a big fight. The groups promptly voted that all moneys go to Cristal. There was no fight. A caucus had been held previous to the meeting where agreement was reached.

Foundation Category

Trick Number 2: Divide and Conquer

A proposal of undisputed merit is submitted to a foundation by a group of Chicanos. The Board of Directors has other priorities for its money, but how does it say NO without getting criticism? The telephone call is a splendid blocking device. The Foundation people call a few Chicano "leaders" in the area from which the proposal writing group springs. They ask for their candid assessment of the group and its ability to administer such a grant. The dirt will fly.

Within a matter of hours the Board should have sufficient reasons—"militant," "vendidos," etc.—to withhold funding and justify its decision with a plausible press release ("This group lacks the confidence of the Mexican American community . . .")

Foundation Category

Trick Number 3: How Much Money Do You Really, Really Need?

Foundations usually don't have a Chicano program. Some haven't ever funded a Chicano project. A Chicano group now requests a fairly sizable grant. What does the foundation do?

It accepts the proposal for study. It calls several meetings to rewrite the proposal and discuss the merits of the program. Close to the time for the final word, the gringo says, "Gentlemen, this budget as presented is high. How much money do you really, really need?" They stand back. The Browns will chop the budget to shreds in minutes. The next question then is, "Well, then. What other items can we deduct?"

Later—if necessary—they will employ Trick Number 2. A few dollars in a Chicano project always brightens up the foundation's PR image ("We're involved, etc.").

Foundation Category

Trick Number 4: Sole Source Funding

Plop, plop, plop . . . that's the sound of Chicano organizations floppin' in the mud in the wake of Tricky Dick's 74–75 budget. Each was securely fastened to only one source of dollars, usually O.E.O. The *patrón* said, "Basta."

If your barrio program is dependent on a single funding source, you are dependent on a single apron string. If you are going to have apron strings, it is better to have many. *Por aquello de las dudas.* Chicano projects have been notorious for failing to expand their funding sources.

The Southwest Council of La Raza for years only danced to the tune of the Ford Foundation. Today, it is practically bankrupt.

Foundation Category

Trick Number 5: Are You Financially Responsible?

When your group seems sure to corner some of a foundation's funds for a community project, they will ask, "Is your organization fiscally responsible?" The phrasing may be a little more sophisticated and roundabout, but that's the message.

They will send a CPA or two over to examine the group's books. You probably won't have any. Now, how could any reasonable person expect a foundation to turn over its scarce funds to such an irresponsible group?

Ask the Texas Migrant Council how many years it took to demonstrate fiscal responsibility.

Foundation Category

Trick Number 6: Let Efrem Zimbalist Handle It

Demonstrations, protests, and boycotts get messy, but quick. Your federal government—and most citizens—take a dim view of them. The Feds have trained agents to arbitrate community disputes of this nature. The now defunct Community Relations Service in the Justice Department is a good example.

Official arbitrators want to restore peace, not solve problems. You can request their help and announce their intervention to the press. It makes good copy. The people will have visions of an even-handed Efrem Zimbalist-type coming down to do good. However, be careful you don't wind up negotiating with the government. Practically every school boycott and walkout suffered from government intervention.

Foundation Category

Trick Number 7: Bring in Papá and Mamá

This is the scene: Chicano kids have been boycotting classes for three days. No end to the walkout is in sight, and the school board finds their demands for bilingual/bicultural education unreasonable: "They've got to learn to be American." The principal has discovered outside agitators from Raza Unida in your quiet but progressive community.

How does the school board get the kids back in school, where they belong? They call the parents to a conference. The parents are more polite and more susceptible to intimidation. The administrators will talk about the serious problems their kids will have in the future without a high school diploma. They talk about how "race" problems were nonexistent before. "Some of my best friends were Mexicans." They will promise to "work" things out as soon as the kids are back in school. The kids will be back in school in a day or two. Those who don't return will be expelled. The boycott is broken because the Chicanos got divided.

Law and Order Category

Trick Number 8: Brown Pigs

Chicanos have long complained about police brutality. The Texas Rangers, the migra, the local pigs are almost always lily-white. When Chicanos protest the brutality and discrimination of the pigs, invariably someone will demand more Chicanos on the police force. Bad mistake.

Chicanos get what they want. Brown pigs must be tougher and meaner than gringos in beating other Chicanos. Now even the *rinches* have a few Chicanos on board.

Job Category

Trick Number 9: Maintenance Engineer?

Ever seen a Mexican buck private? Obviously, you have. How about a general? Chicanos seldom are given the positions of authority.

Many institutions and businesses exploit the Chicano by hiring him for one position and placing him in another. The quota books on Mexicans look good and the wages are kept down.

Job Category

Trick Number 10: Chicano and Chicana

Most employers are besieged today with quotas. They must hire x number of Chicanos, x number of blacks, x number of women. Obviously, if they hired the proportionate number of minorities, few jobs would be left for regular gringos.

The trick then is not to hire a Chicano, a black, and a Chicana— three people.

The employer will hire a Chicana—a female who is Chicano.

Two birds with one stone.

Job Category

Trick Number 11: Humble Humble

Back in 1968, the Humble Oil Corporation was the target of Chicano protests because of its racist hiring practices. Few Chicanos were employed by Humble Oil. And those hired were mostly janitors and clerical help.

At a Raza Unida conference in San Antonio, the participants voted unanimously to boycott Humble Oil. The problem, however, was how to dramatize the issue. The middle-class Chicanos had the answer: tear up the credit card and mail it to Humble. Almost immediately, Humble Oil started hiring accountants, engineers, supervisors, etc.

Political Category

Trick Number 12: On Chicano Politics

LBJ has his Henry B. González; Nixon, his Henry Ramírez; and Ted Kennedy has César Chávez. At the last Democratic convention, the Chicano's problems were dismissed with the slogan "Boycott lettuce." The Republicans gobbled tons of lettuce but paraded a covey of Spanish-speaking officials before the TV audience, on cue.

What does all this mean to a hard-working politician? Adopt a Chicano "leader" today. Confine your sporadic activities in the Spanish-speaking arena to boosting his visage and program. Remember the issue is lettuce, not jobs, housing, civil rights, nor equal educational opportunity.

Political Category

Trick Number 13: A Chicano Is a Chicano Is a Chicano

Hasn't a Chicano ever confronted you[6] who insists he is not a Chicano? He asserts and defends loudly that he's an American. The Nation-

---

[6]Chicanos once were also Mexican American, Latin American, Spanish, French, Indian, and a few Greeks.

al Hispanic Finance Committee promoted a fundraiser[7] in Washington, D.C., on September 29, 1972, at $100,000 a couple for Nixon's "Four More Years" Committee to Reelect the President. This committee sought to raise one million dollars and thereby raise the image of the CHICANO to that of HISPANO and to that of AMERICAN.

The following day the *Washington Post*'s Elizabeth Mehren wrote of the event, and the headline read: "Frijoles and Nixon."

To the gringo, a *frijol* by any other name is still a *frijol*.

Keep truckin'.

Job Category

Trick Number 14: Equal Job Employment

The Del Monte Corporation is feeling the heat of charges that its upper echelon, supervisory personnel policy is anti-Chicano. So Del Monte is seeking Chicanos to apply for jobs. All Del Monte wants is the application.

This great multinational corporation wants to demonstrate "Affirmative Action"—the new rhetoric—to show that they are an equal opportunity employer. They never hire anybody. Their Affirmative Action is a farce. They have no intentions of hiring any Chicanos. But they do have a drawer full of applications to show they are trying.

Job Category

Trick Number 15: "Sorry, We're Not Hiring"

Minority persons apply for jobs and are told, "There are no openings. We're not hiring."

This was the situation at Humble Oil. they didn't need any Chicanos to fill their quota. It was full. Besides, the few Chicanos hired are at the bottom rungs of the corporate structure. This way the gringos can continue in the positions of power and control.

---

[7]The fundraiser was called "Tequila Tontería." *¿Qué tantos tontos?*

Miscellaneous

Trick Number 16: "It's Filled"

Apartment hunting and apartment getting are very different if you are not gringo. We tried this experience at A&I in 1966. We would find a notice of an apartment for rent in the newspapers. There would be a telephone number to call. A person with an Anglo-sounding voice and an Anglo-sounding name, like Hoffman or something, would make the call.

"I am calling about the apartment you advertised. How much? Where?" then, "Can I look at it?" "Sure," says the apartment owner, thinking Anglo all the way.

Then, we would send a Chicano or a black to inspect the apartment. The apartment owner, thinking Anglo all the way, would be confused and upset and get around to saying, "I just rented it . . . that's right . . . while you were coming over. I'm sorry," and so on.

To complete the experiment, another Anglo-sounding voice would call up the same apartment owner about the same apartment and ask, "I'm not too late, is the apartment rented yet?" and the owner would say, "No, it's still for rent."

What they mean when they advertise those apartments for rents is "NO MEXICANS." It's against the law to say it or to write it, but not against the law, apparently, to mean it.

Education Category

Trick Number 17: En Loco[8] Parentis

After a confrontation or walkout, or a boycott, the school administration or negotiators for the school board sometimes will try to implement a theory of "en loco parentis."

This is a Latin expression that means exactly "in place of the parents." According to the theory, when the parents aren't around, the school officials can act as parents would if they were on hand. But this is not what the school officials understand the theory to mean when

---

[8]Loco—crazy.

their school is getting trashed. Students, young adults, and children are minors; they are inferior; they cannot be accountable for their actions. Furthermore, they are raising hell. The officials say, "We cannot deal with these mere young people who are the offenders. The discussions must take place with the parents of the offenders." The trick here is to deal with the parents because they are the types of Mexicans the gringos have been used to dealing with in the past.

So, "in place of parents" turns out to mean the opposite: "in place of these wild Mexican kids."

Which is quite a trick.

Negotiation Category

Trick Number 18: "One by One"

In situations such as we have seen in Pecos, Presidio, and El Paso, Chicanos are very strong because they are very together. They help each other. Gringos look at all of those yelling bunch of wild Mexicans and realize they can't be dealt with like that. So the gringos pick the troublemakers out, get their names, especially the ones who seem to be leaders (but you never can be quite sure who the leaders are), and then call them in for a talk, one by one.

"What's wrong with you, boy?"

"Don't you know you're ruining your future?"

"Who's been agitating you people?"

And so on.

Here is the trick. Take a fish out of water and it dies. Take the demonstrator out of the demonstration and he loses his balls.

It doesn't always work.

Demonstration Category

Trick Number 19: "You're Not Going to Graduate"

The trouble goes on. The school administration is getting desperate. The officials won't give in and the trouble won't go away. If Trick Number 18 doesn't work, the gringos try another trick. Students are threatened where they are most vulnerable. Their grades. Of course!

Students making trouble start making zeroes every day. The principal calls them into the office.

"You know that if you keep up this trouble-making, you are not going to graduate."

This business of 'you might not graduate' sits very heavy with a high school senior who may be thinking of going to college in order to learn the technical skills to help run Aztlán.

It is a naked threat. Stop the trouble and you graduate. Keep up the trouble and you don't graduate.

This is called a liberal education.

Demonstration Category

Trick Number 20: "The B-52s"

In case Tricks Number 18 and 19 do not work, as in U.S. foreign policy, you just destroy the enemy. You send in the B-52s. That is what the school administration eventually finds it has to do. It has to flunk the troublemakers in order to get them out of the school legally. It is going on in Pecos right now. It has gone on in Cristal. In fact, it has gone on in all of the thirty-nine walkouts I am familiar with in Texas in the years 1968–1970.

You can bet on it. They'll send in the B-52s. They'll do anything to keep from dealing with these blazing mad and smart Chicano students.

The trick is it's a trick at all. It's straight, cruel power.

Political Category

Trick Number 21: "Disturbing the Election"

The police don't like demonstrations because they don't like Chicanos. The police will try to break up demonstrations if they can. Because the demonstration is legal, they will have to make something you are doing appear to be illegal. They will provoke a situation; they will harass you; then, when you stand up for your rights, they will hang a "disturbing the peace" rap on you . . . for "disturbing the election."

I got nailed with "disturbing the election" in 1972 when I went to vote. I was simply trying to vote. While I was trying to vote, I got involved in a hassle with the election judge about why he was throwing out our Raza Unida poll watchers, who were legally there, and he was illegally throwing out. The judge didn't like that. Hell, he didn't like me. So he called the police. The police came and they couldn't find any law I was breaking, so they invented a new law and charged me with violating it. This is the law about "disturbing the election."

They sure got me out of that polling place for a while, which is what this trick is all about.

Demonstration Category

Trick Number 22: "Parading Without a Permit"

When you are a police officer, you will find any kind of charge to nail Chicanos with. Some students in Cristal were milling around in the street outside one of the schools. They were arrested for disturbing the peace, although whatever peace there was in the street was undisturbed as far as I could see.

In Kingsville, Texas, a little while later, knowing what happened to their Cristal friends, some Kingsville students decided to stay out of the streets. They stayed on the sidewalk. It turned out that the police didn't like them on the sidewalk any more than Cristal police liked students in the street. That's the point. The police don't like Chicano students, period. Anywhere. So the police decided to arrest them and later charged them with "parading without a permit." And the students weren't even having a parade.

Law and Order Category

Trick Number 23: A Student Is a Student?

Any extra-legal police business against Chicanos who are not acting right is just pure harassment. Consider this:

At UTEP[9] in December 1972, campus police arrested Chicano student leaders, members of Raza Unida and MEChA, on the charge

---

[9]University of Texas at El Paso.

that they had failed to identify themselves. Well, thought the students, "We are students; we have business on this campus, which is getting an education; we are walking from one class to another. Why should we have to identify ourselves or submit to questioning when all we are doing is walking from one class to another?" That was their idea, which they learned in social studies, probably. The police do not take social studies. If they want to bust you, they will find a way, even if you are only going to your next class.

This is called harassment.

Law and Order Category

Trick Number 24: The No-Bill Verdict

Sometimes citizens and newspapers and community organizations just can't stand it. They come right out and charge the police with brutality. The charged police officers then are brought before a grand jury. The prosecutor presents the evidence against them and examines them about the events in the charge. The grand jury then thinks about the evidence for about twenty minutes and says "No bill." Since the grand jury has acted positively on this evidence, further legal action against the police officers is impossible; to try to charge them again in some other way subjects them to "double jeopardy." "No bill" means there is not enough evidence to render an indictment. "No bill" really means: Police brutality is okay.

You find this in police brutality cases in Brownsville, where a sixteen-year-old boy had been killed by the police; in San Antonio, where nine Chicanos were killed by police in one year; in Robstown and Dallas, where teenagers were killed. It was "no bill" all the way.

We are not talking about policemen slapping a kid or knocking someone around. We are talking about murder.

Job Category

Trick Number 25: "You're Fired"

The best way to fire a teacher is not to renew his contract. The teacher thinks when this happens, "That's it." And that is what he is supposed to think. The teacher often does not know he has administrative relief available to him. He can demand a hearing at which he will be presented with the specific accusation against him, and then he can defend himself against the accusation. If the board hears this and then upholds the original firing, the teacher doesn't have to drop the matter. He can appeal the adverse ruling to the commissioner of education. And if the commissioner turns him down, he can go into the courts and sue to get his job back.

So far as I know, only one Chicano teacher has gone the whole way in protesting his termination. The teacher, Josué Garza of Uvalde, went right into the federal courts and tried to get his job back. He lost. He couldn't prove that he had been fired willfully. All he could do was point out that he had been teaching in that district for seven years, without any accusation of incompetence. Then he decided to run for public office. Worse luck: he ran on the Raza Unida ticket. Probably the courts can't understand anything that simple or blatant.

Yes, you can contest being fired.

Yes, you probably will stay fired.

Foundation Category

Trick Number 26: Matching Money

You submit a proposal to a foundation. You need $60,000. The foundation answers, "We really like you and we are committed to you and what you stand for, but we cannot release money to you immediately." The foundation will tell you, "Here is what we are prepared to do. We will match the money you can raise from other sources. We don't want you to be dependent on us alone," or some other such lie.

In effect, you have a blank check that you can't cash because it has no amount written in and it isn't signed. Until you pick up some matching money some place else, of course. You are caught in a predicament. You've got an apparently responsive foundation, but you need someone else to put in the actual first money, and that is the only money the foundation will match. So you need $60,000 from this foundation, and you find you can raise only $5,000 from another source. The foundation cheerfully comes across with a matching

$5,000 and congratulations. You need $60,000; you've actually got $10,000 plus some congratulations. They are still good guys; you are short $50,000.

You've been tricked. They didn't give you enough money to operate with.[10]

Foundation Category

Trick Number 27: Screw the Other Guy

A favorite trick of foundation executives is to get you to believing they are going to give you some money. Sometime in the conversation they are going to ask you in a serious vein to explain your real relationship to another organization, your real feelings. "How does your grant activity relate to what other Chicano organizations are doing?"

Here is what they want you to do: They want you to screw your hermanos. They want you to answer, "Those other people are no good. We are better than they are. We are the real Chicanos. We are doing the real business with Chicano people."

The foundation executives' eyes light up to hear you say that. Later, when they get together with other foundation executives,[11] they say among themselves that "Chicano organizations do not get along. They bitch about each other all of the time."

When you are asked a question that forces you to lie or to gut another Chicano organization, you've been tricked. Your best answer is to hit the sonofabitch in the nose.

Foundation Category

Trick Number 28: "You're Too Political"

This is what foundations finally get around to saying, after they have decided not to fund you. They say, "You're too political." Only activist groups are charged with being too political. Foundations give millions of dollars to colleges and universities, and I have never heard

---

[10]See Trick Number 3.
[11]The executives of foundations get together regularly. They are not in competition. Never forget that.

of one of them being questioned about their political involvement. Even though they are political as hell. Anti-war student demonstrations in the early stages of the Nixon administration made exactly this point. Government research grants, foundation research grants are political. Research does not stop at the edge of politics. Some of the things done in the name of research are political.

The Southwest Research Laboratory in San Antonio ran a program in which dummy birth control pills—placebos—were given to Chicano women who thought they were taking birth control pills and acted accordingly. That was a political act against our Raza, but not the same as research programs, apparently. You can tell that because only activist groups are called too political and are denied funds for that reason.

In 1968, MAYO had a program for community development, community organization, and community encouragement. Anything to strengthen Chicanos. We were activist but not political. The Ford Foundation, which funded the Southwest Council, which funded the Mexican American Unity Council, which funded MAYO, said MAYO was too political and threatened to cut everybody's funds off if MAYO didn't stop being political. That was easy for us. All we had to do was stop doing what we had never started.

Political Category

Trick Number 29: "You're Raza Unida, Aren't You?"

If you get past Trick Number 28 and establish that you are not too political, then you will find you are charged with being a part of Raza Unida. Foundations evidently think that is something like having cancer. TIED—the Texas Institute for Educational Development—suffered through a lot of this insinuation because some of its people were members of La Raza Unida. The same thing had happened to MAYO and the Committee for Rural Democracy, which is a nationwide community organizing type of organization. It suffers the stigma of Raza Unida association. Some of its personnel belong to the party, even though its board is highly representative of all sectors of the American society. That doesn't make any difference. Some of the personnel are Raza Unida members, so the whole organization is suspect.

Nobody else is questioned about his or her politics as a precondition for getting a foundation grant. A college doesn't lose its grant because of the politics of its president. A research proposal is not made to stand or fall on the basis of the politics of its laboratory technician.

But Chicanos and their organizations are questioned about their politics, and if they are Raza Unida politics, they had better stop looking for foundation money.

Political Category

Trick Number 30: "Starving You Out"

I have seen applications to the federal government turned down for one reason only, that Raza Unida runs the cities that made the applications. There are few cities run by Raza Unida, so it is easy to check out. The Texas cities of San Juan, Cotulla and Crystal City have submitted applications, all of which were turned down for the same reason. No other city gets turned down for being Democratic or Republican. Of course, there may be some negotiations called for if you are a Democratic-controlled city trying to get federal funds from a Republican administration. But the negotiations are possible, especially if you are applying for services, such as health care, or reading programs, or surplus food. These services go beyond politics, and the party in power ordinarily grants ordinary applications from any party. Except if you are Raza Unida.

It's an old trick. It is called "starving you out."

Law and Order Category

Trick Number 31: Militant

This is a word trick. A definition trick. Words are loaded with values. By using certain words, you define whole situations as well as label certain persons.

Ramsey Muñiz has a good story to tell about this trick. Ramsey was running for governor in Texas, but he was labeled "the candidate of the militant Raza Unida Party." Ramsey sued the *San Antonio Express* for a large amount of money. Here is the basis of his suit: he argues that by being labeled as a militant, he was precluded from having access to a certain large sector of the voting population. Many people in this sector think a militant is somebody who is about to throw some dynamite into their front rooms or take over the government by force. He said that the Republican party was not called the Fat-Cat Republican party, or the Democratic Party the Labor Union-Controlled Democratic Party. But Raza Unida was called the militant Raza Unida Party. He argues this is a vicious double standard.

The judge who heard the suit was either a Republican or Democrat and certainly not Raza Unida and couldn't see what all the fuss was about. He redefined the word militant. It doesn't mean somebody prepared to use military means to achieve political goals, the judge said. Militant means someone who is a hard worker, aggressive, a go-getter. "What's so bad about that?" he asked.

There wouldn't be anything bad about that, and Ramsey would not have filed the suit if that was what the word militant really means to everybody else in the state of Texas except that judge who happened to be hearing Ramsey's suit.

Negotiation Category

Trick Number 32: No Chairs

This happened in Cristal. We went to a school board meeting one night in the fall of 1969—that is, before the great walkout. Lo and behold, there were no chairs in the room for citizens, only chairs for board members.

This is a trick. It depends on a practical observation of how people behave in public. If you go to a dance or a meeting or to church, you always try to fit yourself into a chair as far from the front of the room as possible. And if there are no chairs, you will stand around the back of the room. Right?

This night the board expected us to come into the room from the back, see that there were no chairs, and just sort of pile up in the back of the room and get nervous and uncomfortable and crowded.[12]

---

[12]The trick didn't work. We crowded around, all right. We crowded around the board, and sweated and talked Spanish, and scared the hell out of them. After that, the board had chairs.

Demonstration Category

Trick Number 33: "What's Your Name, Boy? Where Do You Work?"

Jesús Ramírez confronted Judge Richardson of Hidalgo County, Texas, with a request that he improve the food stamp and welfare programs of the county. Jesús was there with about thirty ladies, and they presented a petition to the judge. Jesús was eighteen years old. The judge didn't like him and didn't like Mexicans coming into his court trying to upset the government. So the judge asked Jesús, "What's your name, boy?"

Anybody who knows a thing about harassment knows that this question is the first part of a two-part series of questions. He doesn't want to know only your name. Your name alone doesn't mean a thing. He wants to know your name so that he can put pressure on you at your job.

Sure enough, the next words out of the judge's mouth were, "Where do you work?" This question means, "If I know where you work, I can go down to your employer or call him up and find out if the employer knows what you're up to, boy."

Jesús said that his name was not at issue. He wouldn't tell the judge his name because Jesús wanted better welfare in Hidalgo County. The judge had him arrested on the spot and thrown in jail, for "disturbing the welfare," one guesses.

Demonstration Category

Trick Number 34: "Who's Your Spokesman?"

You finally get on the agenda at an important meeting. You have gotten by Trick Number 69. You are relieved. Now you are going to get to tell the gringos where to go. The agenda item is called for. That's your group. And when it is your turn, three or four people start to talk all at once. Most groups are disorganized. They haven't had the foresight to choose one person who will be the spokesman and who will say it all. So there you are, three or four talking at once, and the gavel falls. You stop talking. The chairman says:

"Who's your spokesman? We can't listen to everybody talk at once. Can't you people ever agree on who'll speak for you?"

Negotiation Category

Trick Number 35: The Good Old Friendly Department of Justice on Your Side Trick

The federal Department of Justice has a Community Relations Service. It is funded ostensibly for a particular function: to defuse potentially dangerous, explosive community situations. Here are even-handed, fair, experienced people. They will talk to both sides and work out a solution to the explosive situation.

Forget that. In every situation I know of, the CRS negotiates for the standard gringo community against the Chicano or black activists. They don't want to solve the problem, which has become so explosive. Their concern is to stop the immediate trouble. The Chicanos think, "It must be fair, because these are people from the federal government and not ordinary gringo pigs." This is Department of Justice awe. This is the FBI, Efrem Zimbalist as Jesus Christ, and he is right there in front of you. You bet he is. And he is suckering you out of your valid and explosive interest.

The trick is to make you think there is a big difference between CRS and local police. There isn't.

Political Category

Trick Number 36: He Can't Read

It's time to vote. You know how you want to vote. You want to vote a straight ticket: Raza Unida all the way. But you can't read. If there is no Raza Unida poll watcher in that polling place, you might as well walk right back out and not vote at all. If you say "I can't read," the election judge will treat you like a wolf treats lambs. He will give you the assistance you need. You will say "straight Raza Unida ticket," and he will make damned sure it is straight Democratic.

Laws and Order Category

Trick Number 27: "Do Your Job or Go to Jail"

It happened in Laredo. Some Raza Unida poll watchers were doing their job. They were reading ballots clearly marked straight Raza Unida, and they were hearing the judge read the ballots as straight Democratic party votes. It didn't seem possible the election judge could make such a bad mistake in reading, so the poll watchers challenged the ballots and refused to let the judge count the ballots in their tally. The election judge said to them, "If you all continue to tell me what I can't do, I'll call the police and have you arrested. We can't have you all disrupting the election."

If the poll watchers do their jobs, and watch the polls, and make challenges of improper or illegal activities, they go to jail.

If the poll watchers do their jobs and challenge the judge any-more—he has a free ride without them in the polling place.

The election judges really mean: Do your job and go to jail.

Political Category

Trick Number 38: "Here Come the Judge"

In 1972 during the general election in Cristal, Eliseo Soliz was certified as a Raza Unida poll watcher and assigned to the precinct-polling place located in the county courthouse. He was a school-teacher, had been in Cristal only three months, and was new to Raza Unida. This was his first election, so he volunteered to be a poll watcher. He went to poll watcher school. There he heard, dozens of times, "Don't leave the polling place under any circumstances, because if you leave, you're not going to get back in."

He showed up with other Raza Unida poll watchers. The election judge decided he didn't want seven Raza Unida poll watchers, even though every one of them was properly certified. The judge wanted only one. He told six of them to leave. One of these six was Eliseo. He remembered his instructions, however. He knew he wasn't sup-posed to leave. So he refused the order of the judge. The judge called the sheriff. The sheriff came over and arrested him, and still Eliseo wouldn't leave. It took several strong deputies to get him out of that polling place and over to the county jail.

He spent three hours in jail on election day. He still feels he did a bad job as a poll watcher. After all, he let a carload of armed deputy sheriffs carry him off to jail.

Political Category

Trick Number 39: Prove Your Citizenship

You walk into the polling place. You are going to vote. You announce your name and address. The election judge does not welcome you or say hello before showing you to the booth. He asks you to prove your citizenship.

Or, you are walking down the street and you get deported to México because it is pretty clear you are a Mexican. Just like that. Just because you can't prove your citizenship.

I'll bet you ten-to-one that the average American at any given time on any given day would be hard pressed to prove his citizenship for the main reason that the average American doesn't carry his birth certificate around with him.

Chicanos in this part of the country are selectively picked up and asked to produce their citizenship proof on the spot, then and there, because where we live is close to México. However, I notice that Canadians don't have that kind of trouble living in Buffalo, New York. Canadians look like average gringos.

Puerto Ricans don't have that kind of trouble on the East Coast, either, because Puerto Rico is part of the United States. But if a Puerto Rican comes down here to South Texas, and he just lands in San Antonio, for instance, he is going to be picked up sooner or later because now, with his brown skin and his talking Spanish and all, he is going to look like a Mexican.

The trick is to keep that line clear. Even native-born Americans of Mexican descent are very good Americans and are always suspect.

Political Category

Trick Number 40: "We Ran Out of Ballots"

Some particular precincts in San Antonio and Laredo (both big Democratic machine cities) always run out of ballots, every election. They never have done the right preparation. They have not correctly anticipated the number of voters. It is interesting that they never anticipate too high. Always too low. So the election officials conveniently run out of ballots at the very time when the trend of voters seems to be running against their favorite candidates and they feel they might lose.

It is all so plausible. The people standing in line wanting to vote are told they can't vote. "Y'all gonna have to come back later," they are told. Some other election, maybe.

Political Category

Trick Number 41: The Machine Doesn't Work

This is Trick Number 40 in precincts that have voting machines instead of paper ballots. In these precincts that use voting machines, there are times during the election when the machine gets jammed and can't be used. The machine doesn't work and it is announced to be inoperative. This never happens, interestingly enough, until after the election officials feel confident that they already have enough votes registered on the machine for their favored candidates. When they have a certain victory, then the machine gets jammed.

It is the late afternoon; Raza Unida voters are pouring in. But they can't vote. The machine doesn't work. "Come back next election," they are told.

Political Category

Trick Number 42: Machines Don't Always Tell the Truth

In San Antonio during the 1972 general election, Chicano voters came charging into the polling places all worked up to vote on electronic machines for their champion candidate for governor, Ramsey Muñiz. The election officials saw all of that dedication and confusion with the machines. They asked, "You want to vote for Ramsey Muñiz?" The voters said "Sure." The officials said, "Okay. Vote here." The voters did.

"Here" was the lever for a straight Democratic ticket vote.

Political Category

Trick Number 43: "Prove You Are a Citizen"

In an election the authorities are not going to ask you for your citizenship proof before allowing you to vote. They ask you in order to keep you from voting. "Prove you are a registered voter," they say. Well, your proof is that you have a voter registration certificate.

People going to vote don't have to have a voter registration certificate to vote, but they don't know that. So when they are asked for their certificate and they say, "I don't have it with me," they are immediately told, "You can't vote."

Here is the real situation. The election judge has to waive your producing the actual voter registration certificate if you will sign an affidavit that says that you are properly registered and that your certificate has been lost, stolen, or destroyed by accident. But you can't sign an affidavit that says you are careless and forgot to bring your certificate. That is why the judge will try to get you to say that you haven't got it. He wants to discourage you. He knows that not many people are committed and patriotic enough to come to vote twice. If you can't vote right now and have to go home and go through all your stuff, find the certificate, then come back, you probably won't come back.

"Prove you are a voter" really means "don't vote."

Political Category

Trick Number 44: "Here Come the Judge Again"

Experienced poll watchers are vital to your chances of winning an election. Election judges, therefore, hate experienced Raza Unida poll watchers. Mexicans are not supposed to be that smart about what the law actually says. So the trick is to get rid of the poll watchers, or as many of the poll watchers as possible.

As we saw in Trick Number 38, the election judge tried to throw out six of the seven Raza Unida poll watchers. He could do this by misreading one of the three sections of the Texas Election Code dealing with poll watchers. In order to come to his strange decision, he had to ignore completely the other two sections.

Well, the experienced poll watchers quoted these two sections of the code for him. When they did that, the judge did not thank them. He called the sheriff. The sheriff said, "I'm not here to interpret the law. I'm here to enforce the law. And what the judge here says is the law."

Political Category

Trick Number 45: "Clerk For Us"

Sophisticated election judges don't like crack poll watchers any more than blatant racist election judges do. But the sophisticated judges do something different. They don't want you to hassle them all day long, so they ask you to "clerk for us." They try to co-opt you. "We have a lot of work," they say. "Why not help us out?" And, unthinking, you are pleased to get along so well with the gringos and not have that entire hassle. Look out!

Once you start being a clerk, you stop being a poll watcher. You are busy doing a clerk's job. You are part of the election team. You can't challenge. You can't keep an eye on things. You can't protest. You are "gringo for a day." You have been tricked.

Let gringos do gringo dirty business. You do the poll watching. Some day you may have won some elections and appointed your own election judges who are fair. Then you can be a clerk.

Foundation Category

Trick Number 46: "Aren't You Cheerful Brown People Happy?"

Foundations often ask 'how much money do you really need?' The trick word is *really*. So when you are asked in public any question with really in it, beware. When people want to embarrass you in public, they will question your platform, your program, your history, and your priorities with a question like: "What do you *really* want?"

The question means that all of your answers are phony, and you are hiding something. They want to know, "Why are you doing all this?"

You can check it out for yourself. Every time people ask you that kind of question, they are disguising another, and the other question is, "Aren't you cheerful brown people happy?"

Job Category

Trick Number 47: "How About a Job?"

Okay, the attempts to destroy you haven't worked, and the later attempts to co-opt you haven't worked, either. Now it is clear you are going to continue to be a crazy Mexican. Get ready. Next, the system is going to offer you a job—maybe even a good, high-paying job. It is a bone they are offering you, to keep you from eating them up.

This trick has worked sensationally in urban areas such as Houston, Dallas, and San Antonio. You can go into those places and find all kinds of tigers who are now pussycats. They are working for the system. The government agencies are where you can find a lot of them. But you can find them in other places of little importance, doing some job, which is fooling or screwing the people.

They fall for the trick, obviously. Lots of them are now beginning to see that it is a trick because they are losing their jobs. Nixon is making militants and revolutionaries out of previously chicken-livered OEO bureaucrats. He has had the nerve to fire them. They are now ashamed at how they were tricked.

Law and Order Category

Trick Number 48: "Are You Getting Smart?"

It is a demonstration. You are there, all steamed up and ready to go. The police are there, and they are all steamed up to keep you from going. Their trick is to make you into a bad guy. They are coming in to arrest you. They set you up. They take advantage of how excited and tense you are. They insult you. And the minute you say something back to them, they say the unanswerable words, "Are you getting smart?"

No matter what you answer, you're wrong. Right? You say "no," and they take that as argument, as proof that you are getting smart. If you say "yes," you have conceded their point, and, anyway, who would answer "yes" to that question? You are wrong, no matter how you answer. You are, in fact, under arrest.

Law and Order Category

Trick Number 49: The Importance of the Pretrial Examination

I have been reading rural newspapers for years. In all this time I have yet to find an account of a Chicano who didn't waive his right to a pretrial examination. This is the most important pretrial event. Here you are going to discover what the police have against you by way of evidence, and you also learn how the prosecuting attorney is going to present the case. You can build your defense out of what you learn in that examining trial.

The Chicanos I have read about have waived this crucial event, to a person, and you can guess that the trials went off without a hitch. They were found guilty. These rural county attorneys have a fantastic record of convictions. The reason their records look so great is simple. They have talked the defendants out of their basic rights and, thus, made it almost certain the Chicanos are going to be found guilty. It is easy when you know how.

Law and Order Category

Trick Number 50: No Bond

If you are arrested, you will find that you are going to have a lot of trouble getting bond. The sheriff, who doesn't like you, is going to be tough. Only the sheriff has the discretion of approving bond signatures, in case you don't happen to have a whole pocketful of cash on you at the time. The sheriff is not going to accept any old signature. He wants the signatures on your bond to be the signatures of respectable citizens who own property, whose names currently are on the tax rolls. That makes a person respectable.

Few Chicanos own property, so few Chicanos are on the tax roll. The sheriff has the discretion to turn all these Chicano signatures down, no matter how long he has known them or you. It is a trick. It is another way to tell you he hates you.

Law and Order Category

Trick Number 51: "Two Million Dollars"

If you are arrested, and it looks like there is a Chicano, as a matter of fact, who has property on the tax rolls and is ready to sign your bond, the sheriff still is not without a trick. He can set the bond at a tremendous figure, so high that there is no way you can meet it. He could say "$50,000." It might as well be two million, no matter what he says, because it is going to be such a big number you can't reach it.

The next day you can go in to the judge and ask him to lower the bond to a reasonable figure, and the law forces him to do it, but for awhile, you are at the sheriff's mercy and in jail.

Political Category

Trick Number 52: No Spanish Speaking

The Texas election law is in the process of being changed, and one of the changes we have forced is the provision that makes it illegal to speak Spanish in a polling place. No matter if the election law is changed, you can bet that election judges will try to enforce the old law as though the law hadn't been changed.

Election laws prohibit dialogue in Spanish between voter and poll watcher or voter and clerk. If you can't speak English, or you speak it poorly, you naturally are going to speak Spanish to whomever in there can understand you. And that person begins to act as your interpreter. As soon as that happens, the election judge says, "No Spanish speaking in here!" He says, "I'll do the talking from now on. All right, talk up. You wanna vote? You know how to read? You know how to write?" And so on. He begins to harass the voter in English about his not knowing English, and, sure enough, the trick works. The voter comes unglued. He ends up not voting or voting wrong.

You can change the law from now on, and still, gringo election judges will try to use this trick.

Job Category

Trick Number 53: Friendly Persuasion

It is voting day. Your employer makes it clear to you that he wants you to vote. He makes it also clear how he wants you to vote. Not content with owning your soul and body, he wants to steal your franchise, too. He makes it clear that if you vote wrong, it doesn't make any difference how good an employee you are, don't come back tomorrow.

The trick is to make you believe he can find out how you have voted. He really can't, but just his saying so seems to mean he has secret ways of finding out how you have voted. It is intimidation. And even if he cannot find out, he is still intimidating you.

Job Category

Trick Number 54: More Friendly Persuasion

You've been in a lot of protests, demonstrations, walkouts, picket lines, boycotts, haven't you? Did you ever wonder why there is always somebody there who is taking pictures of you? It is a way of verifying that you were doing these terrible things to American society. Then, whoever takes the pictures shows them to your employer. The employer then says—to you—"You're fired."

In Cristal, two of the walkout leaders in 1969 lost their jobs the very afternoon of the walkout. Instantly. They weren't given any reason. They were in the walkout, weren't they? They were leaders, weren't they?

The community responded with a boycott of the businesses. The trick is that businesses responded instantly. They fired the protesters.

Demonstration Category

Trick Number 55: Wait Awhile; It'll Go Away

The classical response to an explosive situation is to do nothing, to wait awhile because it will go away. That has been proven wrong, but it is still a dangerous trick.

It is based on the assumption that Chicanos are unorganized and unorganizable. And if they are organized, it will only last a little while, and they'll come apart. Consequently, the best way to defeat this trick is to reverse the assumptions. Instead of coming at them with 100 protesters on the first day, then dwindling off to forty and thirty as the week ends, start with thirty, and work up to 100 at the end of the week. This breaks their theory all to hell and it sets up another notion in the gringo head, which is, "Hell, this is no protest, this is a revolution." They've seen the first thirty, then forty, then 100 crazy Mexicans out there. By the time they see 100, their mind has already transformed the 100 into 1,000.

You've used his trick to trick him.

See Trick Number 133.

Demonstration Category

Trick Number 56: The No-Decision Decision

Wise, confrontation-hardened managers of the system have determined that their best course in explosive situations is, "don't do anything." They decide not to decide. When, therefore, you start attacking the system, challenging an administrator, or making demands on behalf of our Raza, they make no response at all. That is like pushing Jell-O uphill. You push here and it gives there, and you just can't get it up.[13] This, too, is a trick. It is the gringo's way of not giving you any kind of importance, of not giving you an issue, not giving you a reaction, which you can use as an issue.

Demonstration Category

Trick Number 57: Didn't We Tell You?

The opposition calls a very important and controversial meeting. Your group immediately passes the word, begins research, and organizes a group. On the appointed day and time, you arrive at the meeting place. Nobody is around. After some two or three hours and desperate phone calls, you locate an informed source from the opposition.

---

[13] Also a famous bedroom expression.

He says, "Oh, didn't we tell you? The meeting was canceled."
Will your followers come again?

Demonstration Category

Trick Number 58: Didn't You Hear?

Often, Trick 57 is changed to read, "Oh, didn't you hear? So many people were expected, we moved the meeting to another location."

Political Category

Trick Number 59: Can't Run—You Ain't Got the Hours

Every high school and college student at one time or another wants to run and win some campus election. The same is true for Chicanos.

Schools, however, have a better idea. They make the requirement for candidacy a bit stringent. The idea is to eliminate the less serious prospects. The result is Chicano elimination.

You're a sophomore and want to run for vice-president of the student body. You try to file. You are denied. Only those who are juniors or better can run.

What juniors and seniors have that sophs and frosh don't is beyond me. However, we do know that there are fewer Chicanos in the upper-division grades. Could it be this is why the offices are opened at the levels of fewer Chicanos?

Check your local schools and colleges for their requirements.

Political Category

Trick Number 60: Too Small in At-Large

Chicanos must bloc vote only for Chicano candidates and only for the number of Chicanos for which there are positions.

Race A

Three seats are up in an at-large election. You file three Chicanos. You are the minority. You lose. You didn't bloc vote.

Chon Mexicano	20 ch[14] + 0 g	= 20 (lost)
Juan Raza	35 ch + 0 g	= 35 (lost)
José Chicano	30 ch + 0 g	= 30 (lost)
Tom Anglo	12 g[15] + 10 ch	= 22 (lost)
John White	43 g + 10 ch	= 53 (won)
Gary Grey	55 g + 10 ch	= 65 (won)
Bob Bibb	55 g + 20 ch	= 75 (won)

Race B

Three seats are up in an at-large election. You file three Chicanos. You are the minority. You bloc vote. You win one seat after the run-off.

Chon Mexicano	45 ch + 0 g	= 45 (run-off)
Juan Raza	45 ch + 0 g	= 45 (run-off)
José Chicano	45 ch + 0 g	= 45 (run-off)
Tom Anglo	12 g + 0 ch	= 12 (lost)
John White	43 g + 0 ch	= 43 (lost)
Gary Grey	55 g + 0 ch	= 55 (won)
Bob Bibb	55 g + 0 ch	= 55 (won)

Race C

Three seats up in an at-large election. You file four Chicanos. You bloc voted. You lost. You didn't bloc vote for the same three.

Mele Mex	35 ch + 0 g	= 35 (lost)
Chon Mexicano	40 ch + 0 g	= 40 (lost)
Juan Razo	40 ch + 0 g	= 40 (lost)
José Chicano	25 ch + 0 g	= 25 (lost)
Tom Anglo	12 g + 0 ch	= 12 (lost)
John White	43 g + 0 ch	= 43 (won)
Gary Grey	55 g + 0 ch	= 55 (won)
Bob Bibb	55 g + 0 ch	= 55 (won)

---

[14]ch means Chicano.
[15]g means gringo.

Political Category

Trick Number 61: Run-Off or Ran-Off?

The primary election of the major political parties is designed to choose the candidate of the party for the November general election. In Texas, the primary is held on the first Saturday in May. This primary not only helps the political party choose its nominee, but also eliminates Chicano candidates. Most of our people are already migrating to the northern states for agricultural employment by May 1st. And all of yours are gone by June, which is the month that a run-off election is held in the event that no candidate receives a majority of the vote.

Example A (Primary)			Example B (Run-Off)		
Juan Raza	60 ch	(run-off)	Juan Raza	39 ch	(lost)
Joe White	40 g	(lost)	Tom Anglo	158 g	(won)
Tom Anglo	61 g	(run-off)	Total Votes Cast	197	
Gary Grey	57 g	(lost)			
Pancho Pendejo[16]	58 ch	(lost)			
Total Votes Cast	285 (158 g + 127 ch)				

Clearly, Juan Raza lost votes from the primary to the run-off. Obviously, primaries and run-offs need to be avoided by Chicanos. Our candidates should find a way to place themselves on the November ballot when our people are back home and voting. Additionally, in November the winner is the candidate with the most votes and not the majority.

Political Category

Trick Number 62: Vote For or Against

Chicanos have complained bitterly over the lack of choice in elections since time immemorial. Usually, the answer in Trick 66 is used. However, a new trick[17] was employed in Texas during 1970.

---

[16]Pancho Pendejo—There is always a *mexicano* who will split the Chicano vote.

[17]Actually, the trick was previously used effectively in South Vietnam's elections.

The Raza Unida Party sought ballot status in four South Texas counties. Every court in the state, from the county court to the state supreme court, denied access to the ballot.

The final hopes all rested with the federal district court. Our attorneys argued, among other points, that in most Texas counties the only party on the ballot for local elections was the Democratic Party; consequently, the placing of the Raza Unida Party on the ballot would be a real choice for the voters.

The federal judge, a Democrat, clearly explained his concept of choice: "There is a choice for the voters on the existing ballot. They can vote for or against the Democratic Party."

The Raza Unida Party was denied ballot status.

Political Category

Trick Number 63: Joe por José?

After Trick 62 was pushed on the voters of Texas, the Raza Unida Party conducted a write-in campaign. It was disastrous.

Take the example of José Serna, candidate for county commissioner of Precinct 3. José campaigned hard and heavy doing street canvassing and teaching people how to write his name on the ballot. The majority of the voters in the precinct were Chicanos.

Election time came and José Serna lost. The results were published:

José Serna	51
Joe Serna	48
José Cerna	33
Joe Cerna	39
J. Serna	38
J. Cerna	15
Mildred Keller	119

It was the first time the gringo could tell the difference between one Mexican from another.

Political Category

Trick Number 64: No Property—Can't Run

Gabriel Tafolla in 1969 sought election to the city council of Uvalde, Texas. He filed for office and started his campaign. A day before the absentee balloting began, the city attorney announced that Tafolla was ineligible to run for office. Tafolla was not a property owner, as required by the city charter.

Attorneys for Gabriel argued that such a property requirement was unconstitutional. In light of previous U.S. Supreme Court rulings, property ownership could not be a requirement for candidacy. By the time the case was heard and won, the election was under way. Gabriel won his case, but not the election.

Political Category

Trick Number 65: Forfeit the Votes?

The gringos again employed Trick 64 in 1970 against the Raza Unida Party's candidate for the city council of Crystal City: Pablo Puente. He, too, was disqualified on the grounds of lacking property.

The case went to court. Pablo won his case but the judge, as in the Tafolla case, said the ballots were printed, the election was under way and could not be stopped. His attorneys, however, argued that the judge could order ballots immediately. Failure to do so would allow every municipality to disqualify candidates at the last minute. The judge offered a deal: I'll order new ballots printed with your name for election day if you'll forfeit the absentee ballots already cast without your name.

Pablo agreed and won.

On April 3, 1970, the official results were:

Pablo Puente	1306
Ventura González	1341
Charles Crawford	820
Emmett Seville	835

The judge had overlooked the fact that Chicanos seldom vote absentee. Consequently, the votes forfeited were anti-Puente votes, anyway.

Political Category

Trick Number 65: Vote for the Lesser of Two Evils

Elections decide a winner and a loser. But for people without a candidate, elections are always losing propositions.

The masses are extolled to vote for Mr. X because he's better than Mr. Y. Soon enough in the campaign, Mr. X and Mr. Y are indistinguishable in their rhetoric, promises, and bad deeds. The masses are extolled to vote for Mr. X—he's the lesser of two evils.

What a choice! Vote for an unfit candidate because the other choice is more unfit. What happened to voting for a good candidate of the people?

Education Category

Trick Number 67: Missing Agenda

Invariably at a public meeting, someone or some group will request the floor for a presentation. And, invariably, if the petitioners are friendly, they get all the time they need. However, if the petitioners are hostile, then the chairman will quickly lower the boom with the reprisal "You're not on the agenda."

Agendas don't have to be prepared, much less publicized. You should obtain all the information possible on the public body's procedure at public meetings before asking for recognition. Your best weapon is to make them comply with their own rules.

Miscellaneous Category

Trick Number 68: Full Agenda

In similar fashion to Trick Number 67, a chairman's best defense is his ability to juggle the agenda. He may prolong discussion or stop discussion, whatever his whim. He can omit or add to the agenda as he sees fit.

This expert on agendas usually will not deny you the floor. He simply says, "I am eager to hear your comments, but our agenda is full. Thank you."

Miscellaneous Category

Trick Number 69: Two Minutes

"I am eager to hear your comments, but our agenda is full. Can you come back next month for two minutes?"

This is the most sophisticated "no" employed by public bodies. Not only do they pretend they want to listen to you, but make you the troublemaker if you refuse their offer. Therefore, you should, in the absence of a published agenda, inform the chairman early in the meeting of your desire to speak and your willingness to wait until all their matters are taken care of before proceeding to your business.

Miscellaneous Category

Trick Number 70: Wind and Sails

People get nervous when speaking before large crowds. A public official doesn't. His job is performing before large crowds. At public meetings, the officials have the upper hand. Frequently, a nervous petitioner gets carried away with emotion or fright in his presentation. The chairman, in a soothing and calm voice will say, "José, we've known each other a long time. There is no need for this. The door to my office is always open to you people. José, why don't you come by tomorrow and we can talk about it over coffee?"

Your group must be calmer than your enemy. And your group must support your leader in his/her time of weakness.

Education Category

Trick Number 71: Three Days or Three Licks

Playing hooky or cutting classes is a favorite pastime of students. Chicanos, when speaking Spanish on school grounds, are punished. This punishment consists of an option, either three-day suspension or three smacks with the paddle. What would you prefer?

What better way to push a student out of school than by encouraging his absenteeism!

Chicanos should neither accept the three licks nor the three days. The parents and student should demand a hearing with the principal, teachers, and others involved on the merits of the case.

Job Category

Trick Number 72: First Come, First Served

Migrant workers during the spring and summer annually trek north in search of agricultural employment. Their journey takes them to all states in the west, midwest, and northwest. For years, employment was plentiful. Then came the machines. Now, pity the migrant who goes north without a definite commitment from a grower. Many migrants are tricked into thinking that jobs are available. Upon arrival, they are told that the first arrivals got the jobs. And in a very accommodating manner, the grower will offer other employment at lower wages. The migrant family must pack up and leave for parts unknown in search of employment or accept a third-rate pay scale.

Education Category

Trick Number 73: I'm in Seven-Five

Returning migrant families are given another bitter example of the first come, first served trick when enrolling their kids in school.

School districts still avoid charges of segregation and tracking of migrant children by placing the new arrivals together as they register. The schools maintain that placing migrants in existing classes would either retard the class or leave the migrant behind. "He is better off with others like him," they argue.

He is better off among Chicanos. However, he is not better off getting the leftover teachers, materials, supplies, textbooks, classrooms, etc., etc., reserved for the late enrollee. He is not better off being stigmatized as a dummy in seven-five by the straight-A gringo of seven-one. He is not better off living separated from other Chicanos because some are migrants and others are not.

Political Category

Trick Number 74: Teacher Cheerleaders

There are few school districts in the Southwest that do not have a Chicano majority in the student body. The change in the balance came in the mid-1960s. Along with this change in student power came a change in education procedures.

Students normally choose cheerleaders, the pride of football teams. Not so in most Chicano-populated school districts; the teachers elect the cheerleaders.

Very wisely, the teachers always elect only one brown-legged Chicanita cheerleader.

Political Category

Trick Number 75: Twirlers

When it comes to twirlers, the rules of election change. On paper, the change in election procedure is even better: the band members vote for the twirlers. In actuality, the change simply accommodates the numerically superior Anglo student. Chicanos, you see, cannot afford the price of musical instruments and are, therefore, not a large percentage of the band membership. They are, however, compensated with one Chicana twirler annually. One wonders if Chicanos have learned to bloc vote (see Trick Number 139) or if the gringos elect token *cocos*[18] to avoid a charge of "gringos only."

Political Category

Trick Number 76: Football Sweetheart

The 1969 election of a football sweetheart in Cristal, Texas, prompted the school blowout. In previous years, the football players, in similar fashion as the band in Trick Number 74, elected the sweetheart. However, the football team soon contained a majority of Chi-

---

[18]*Coco* is Spanish for coconut. A coconut is brown on the outside and white on the inside.

canos, and the election was entrusted to the Ex-Student Association. This group of graduates required that each candidate's parents have graduated[19] from Cristal High School. Only six Chicanas out of some 600 students qualified as compared to all but one Anglo girl. And only members of the Association could vote. The membership was all gringo, but for three *cocos.*

The Chicano community, however, protested the action and threatened to stop the event if it was carried out. It wasn't.

Political Category

Trick Number 77: Elite of Elites

Students do have the right to vote in some elections. Once candidates file for the student governing body (see Trick 59), the constituency is made up of students. Even in Chicano-populated schools, these student governing boards do not reflect the student body's ethnic composition. Grade requirements and the dropout rate severely reduce the number of potential Chicano candidates.

The reason for so few Chicano student body presidents is that most schools select the president from the students elected to the governing board. The president is the elite of the elite.

Political Category

Trick Number 78: Elections by Majority Vote

Majority vote means the winner obtains half of the total votes cast plus one. This procedure benefits the majority population.

Political Category

Trick Number 79: Elections by Plurality Vote

Plurality vote means the winner obtained more votes than any other candidate. This procedure benefits the minority population.

---

[19]After the Civil War, Blacks were allowed to vote only if their grandparents had voted. This was called the Grandfather Clause.

Political Category

Trick Number 80: Too Long, Too Short

Dress codes now appear in all school board policy handbooks in the nation. These dress codes seek to impose the dressing habits of the establishment. Hair length and dress length is of particular concern to the middle-aged, balding, pot-bellied school board member. Boys' hair must be neat and trimmed, and girls can expose no more than three inches above the knee.

Needless to add, the application of these codes is arbitrary. Hair length regulations have prompted school walkouts across the nation. In Weslaco, Texas, Principal Clyde Greer expelled thirty-four Chicanitos in 1973 for long hair. To date, no Anglo has been expelled. We are led to believe another stereotype: Mexican hair grows longer than gringo hair. Similarly, the girls are made to kneel on the floor and the distance between cloth and floor cannot exceed three inches. Pity the long-legged creature that has more leg up from her knee than the sister whose leg is longer below the knee.

Law and Order Category

Trick Number 81: Scholarships and Protest

With the wave of school protests came prohibitive legislation aimed at students. Demonstrations and protests were made illegal along with other First Amendment freedoms. The clincher, however, was the blow to the student's pocketbook.

If you engage in civil disorder, you lose your academic standing, financial assistance, and future scholarships.

Not bad for a democratic society.

Foundation Category

Trick Number 82: Late Proposal

After months of research and writing, your group comes up with a fairly interesting and innovative project to help Chicanos. Your proposal is sent to the foundations in New York.

A couple of weeks later, you receive a letter. It states: "Thank you for your proposal. You have greatly increased our knowledge of the problems confronting Chicanos. We regret to inform you that your proposal arrived too late for consideration."

Little did you know that foundations review proposals at regular intervals during the year. You need to write that foundation again and request that your proposal be presented the next time around. You may be late for one meeting but you are early for the next round.

Foundation Category

Trick Number 83: Large Proposal

More letters arrive from foundations responding to the proposal in Trick 82. A likely response will be that the proposal has merit, is well written, is a very worthwhile project, and your group is well thought of. However, the budget is too large for their grant amounts. Sorry.

When submitting a proposal, indicate exactly the amount of financial support requested from them. A foundation may not afford one million dollars, but it can supply $10,000. Don't ever change your budget for the worse.

Foundation Category

Trick Number 84: Too Narrow, Too Specific

Many groups engaged in grantsmanship will advise you to be precise, clear, and forthright in your proposal's objectives, purposes, and methods. There is no set rule for writing proposals. Foundations will reject proposals because they are too general and vague or because they are too narrow and specific. Foundations love either-or tactics. Either a proposal is too vague or it is too narrow to suit them.

Therefore, write two proposals so that your ass is covered.

Foundation Category

Trick Number 85: Vague Proposal

See Trick Number 84 to avoid Trick Number 85.

Foundation Category

Trick Number 86: You Need a 501-C-3

Few organizations and even fewer activists know what a "501-C-3" is. I didn't.

It took Tricks 5, 82, 83, 84, and 85 for me to graduate to this one.

The Ford Foundation led the Mexican American Youth Organization around for nearly a year on a proposal, only to be finally denied because we didn't have a "501-C-3." A "501-C-3" refers to a section of the Internal Revenue Code that allows tax exemption to certain not-for-profit organizations. All foundation grantees must have a 501-C-3 status. See a lawyer.

Miscellaneous Category

Trick Number 87: Hire a Fiscal Agent

Prior to the Tax Reform Act of 1969, the 501-C-3s were hard to obtain. Now they are collector's items.

But a newly organized group does not need a 501-C-3 to begin operations or solicit funds. You can get a fiscal agent for your grant. The fiscal agent then submits the proposal and administers the program in his name. You might get him to act on your behalf for a small percentage of the grant, maybe for free! It's up to you to arrange for the safeguards with the fiscal agent in advance of the grant award.

Miscellaneous Category

Trick Number 88: Wrong Forms

After years in the struggle, organizers get overconfident. This is a terrible error. In the course of a fight, you seldom can afford one error.

The Del Monte/Teamster fight of 1970 in Cristal underscores this point. The Teamsters have a sweetheart contract with Del Monte plants around the United States—Cristal is no exception. The Teamster sweetheart contract was to expire on September 1, 1970. We consulted with the people in the union; we consulted with attorneys; and we consulted with each other before taking on the fight. We thought we knew what we were doing. A new union, Obreros Unidos, Independientes, was created. A petition to decertify the union was filed with the National Labor Relations Board. We waited. Finally, word came that our petition was on ordinary paper and must be on a proper form. By the time we got the correct forms and obtained new signatures, the deadline for action had passed. You only had sixty days for the entire process. We lost the fight and got collared with another sweetheart contract for three additional years. Now we look forward to September 1, 1973, to try again.

Miscellaneous Category

Trick Number 89: SBA

To secure a guaranteed loan or grant from the Small Business Administration, numerous forms must be filed; among these is a profit and loss statement. This instrument simply reduces to chart form the economic activity of your business. Usually a profit and loss statement for the SBA is done on a ten-year period. A Chicano businessman's profit and loss statement would not reflect growth but a steady, prolonged period of continued business activity. This is our concept of business: maintain the business. The gringo concept of business is rapid growth and expansion. In other words, drive all others out of business. Therefore, Chicanos flunk the economic activity test of the SBA and fail to obtain the loan.

Miscellaneous Category

Trick Number 90: Cash or Credit

Our people are too poor to obtain standing credit accounts, credit cards, revolving accounts, and credit in general from the gringo businesses. Credit is only available within the Chicano barrio.

The result of not having credit is that one must pay cash.

Obviously then, the credit plan offers a greater buying power than does the cash method. Here's how: a credit card enables you to buy $100 worth of merchandise today and pay a small percentage plus interest within thirty days. The cash plan makes you pay exactly for what you buy—now.

The "haves" can have more while the "have-nots" have less.

Law and Order Category

Trick Number 91: No Income Tax—No Income

The employer deducts the income tax but fails to submit the amount to the Internal Revenue Service. The employee renders his wages on his income tax form and claims his tax refund or credit. The IRS promptly demands payment of the tax or else. Chicanos don't keep check stubs for proof of salary or receive statements of wages earned from employers.

Law and Order Category

Trick Number 92: They Took My House!

The bad villain who foreclosed on a poor couple's home was a character in the silent movie days. He is still around.

R.A. Taylor, ex-city attorney, ex-county attorney, and ex-school attorney of Cristal City, Texas, recently foreclosed on homeowners for failure to pay a premium.

This is how he did it: he gave contracts of sale[20] to the purchasers of the house instead of a warranty deed. The contract called for payment of premiums at precise dates. Failure to pay meant you lost your house.

While the courts find justice, the people have lost their home.

Law and Order Category

Trick Number 93: Chain Link or a Link in the Chain

Trick 92 is the basis for this one. In San Juan, Texas, most people have lost their houses over failure to pay for their fences. That's right, fences.

---

[20]Not really a deed.

An outfit will come by the neighborhood, such as Acme Fence Company of Harlingen, Texas, and offer a chain link fence, at a dollar down and a dollar a week, plus a lien[21] on your property plus interest. It'll take many years at a dollar a week to pay the fence, and the interest will make you pay that fence eight to ten times over. Invariably, a homeowner will not make a week's payment; nothing is said. The homeowner will again forget and not make another payment; again, nothing is said. And it continues until the company produces several "notices of collection," several letters of "final notice," and a statement of delinquent charges to the local court. The court orders the total amount of the contract[22] paid in full at once or lose the property.

Miscellaneous Category

Trick Number 94: Poison, Pesticide, and Pen

A large group of Chicano cotton pickers entered the fields early one morning the summer of 1968 near Santa María, Texas. The cotton field had been sprayed late the previous afternoon with parathion. This chemical is better known as nerve gas[23] and is used against the boll weevil.

Because of a low overcast cloud cover, the chemical did not evaporate until the next day with the sunrise. As the day got hotter, the workers got sicker until all the workers (thirty-eight) were unconscious. Ambulances and police cars carried the poisoned Chicanos to various hospitals for treatment. As soon as they regained consciousness and were able to talk of the affair, the owner gave the pat answer: "I don't know." He got the workers to sign statements allowing him to care for them at his expense. They signed. *¡Qué buen patroncito!*

They signed a statement in English, which was an insurance release. Two of the workers later gave birth to defective children, four

---

[21]A lien is where your property is put as a guarantee for a debt. You can't sell your property unless it is clear of all liens.

[22]The contract called for full payment of the terms and interest. You couldn't pay it ahead of time and save the interest.

[23]Nerve gas causes a disorder of the nervous system, uncontrolled vomiting, skin lesions, and death.

still have skin rot, several have respiratory ailments and nervous disorders, and all paid for the medical attention out of their own pockets.

Job Category

Trick Number 95: I Don't Know, Talk to Pancho[24]

Seldom are Chicanos given authority to formulate and dictate policy. One exception is the area of demotions and dismissals. The boss wants to lay off or terminate two or three employees, so he turns to Pancho and instructs him to use his best judgment and pick the two or three from all the Mexican help. Pancho[25] does.

Most of the time, Pancho does use his best judgment and relieves two or three, who will then appeal the dismissal to the boss. The boss will wash his hands of the affair with the pat answer: "I don't know, talk to Pancho. He's your people's boss. You've always been a good worker for me."

This is a classic divide-and-conquer trick. The good guy is the boss. The Chicanos are angry with Pancho, the bad guy.

Job Category

Trick Number 96: Betabeleros y Pizcadores (Beef Thinners and Pickers)

Frequently in Texas on the Spanish radio program, a listener will hear solicitations for field hands. Those interested in work are given an address or a phone number to follow up. A preliminary investigation will indeed reveal employment opportunities in the northern states, fair wages, housing, and travel advances.

Entire families will sign up with the recruiter, take the kids out of school, board up[26] the house, and leave immediately for northern parts. Upon arrival, they are told that Kiko,[27] the recruiter, is too ambi-

---

[24]Pancho is a shortened version of Francisco.
[25]Most Panchos have a first name and a last name.
[26]Board up a house means literally to nail boards over the doors and windows.
[27]Kiko is another shortened version of Francisco.

tious and kind-hearted, that all the hands needed have already been hired. The migrant family is told that since they are there already, they can work at another job at another salary—lower salary, that is.

The family can accept or go hungry.

Law and Order Category

Trick Number 97: A *mojado*[28] *por cuatro*

The sheriffs of many southwestern counties in the United States are the custodians of Mexican deportees awaiting deportation by the U.S. Immigration Service. In this process, many *mojados* are made to work for their keep. A frequent practice in Gillespie County, Texas, is to farm out the boys at four dollars a day to Mitchell's Cabrito Farm. The sheriff, not the *mexicano*, gets the four dollars.

Law and Order Category

Trick Number 98: Three Party Contracts Aren't a Party

The Chicano family in Trick 96 will learn from that experience. The following year they will again hear the radio announcement and again go check out the offer. This time, they will ask and receive a contract for employment. The contract will spell out wages, working conditions, advance travel, and all other pertinent data.

The family arrives, contracts in hand, and begins to work. Very soon thereafter, a breach of the contract occurs. The wages are lowered, the hot water heater broke and is not repaired, or the crop is not in the condition promised.

The family protests to the farmer about the contract.

The farmer protests that it is not his contract.

The family can accept or go hungry.

The American Crystal Sugar Company and its American Crystal Employment Agency are notorious for this trick on sugar beet workers.

---

[28]*Mojado* means a person who crossed the Rio Grande River into the USA illegally. Who is illegal? A *mexicano* who crosses his river to enter occupied México or the gringo who crosses an ocean to occupy a country?

Law and Order Category

Trick Number 99: Pay on the Contract Price and Not by the Hour

A Chicano family[29] enters into agreement to care and harvest a given crop on a given field. Some money is advanced for travel, food, and incidentals.

The work is begun. More money is advanced for food, gasoline, and incidentals.

The work is finished. First, the "debts" of all the money advanced for food, travel, and incidentals are cleared. Second, the final payment is made, and it is less than the agreed price. Finally, the family accepts or is run off the land and possibly arrested for trespassing.

Law and Order Category

Trick Number 100: Residency

Migrants traveling across the United States, regardless of direction, suffer a common problem: residency. Reforms in the voting laws of most states allow residency for voting to be established in thirty days. However, residency for other privileges—divorce, food stamps, credit, health care, public housing, etc.—calls for a longer period of time.

A Texas Chicano ventures into Idaho and is denied services because he's not a resident. His family is denied services because their residency is the same as their father's. Upon returning to Texas, he can't claim unemployment compensation in Texas because he worked in Idaho. He has to file a claim with Idaho. He can't drive his car with Idaho license plates or fill the prescription from the Idaho doctor. And he must always remember to keep his local selective service board informed of his whereabouts.

Who said, see the USA and leave the driving to us?

---

[29]This is not the same family of 96 and 98.

Miscellaneous Category

Trick Number 101: They Lay Away

Chicano credit[30] is the lay-away plan. A piece of merchandise is bought and placed on lay-away. This means that a weekly or monthly payment is made until the goods are paid and the merchandise received. A receipt is made every time a payment is made so that a customer has many receipts as proofs of payment. And all receipts must be offered as proof of payment before the merchandise is released.

Pity the poor Chicano who has lost a receipt. He must pay additionally or forfeit the merchandise.

Law and Order Category

Trick Number 102: Are You Trying to Get Smart?

Chicanos are law-abiding citizens. From time to time, a Chicano will exceed the speed limit posted on a highway. From time to time, a state highway patrolman will observe and stop a speeding Chicano.

The dialogue will go like this:

Patrolman: Good afternoon. The state of Texas would like to see your driver's license.

Chicano: Okay.

Patrolman, as he jots down information: Mister[31] Rodríguez, you were checked at 80 miles per hour by radar up the road. Is there a legal explanation for your hurry?

Chicano: No.

Patrolman, as he looks into the back of car: The legal and posted speed limit on this highway is 70 miles per hour. It is for your safety and the safety of others that the state of Texas has allowed this speed. Why were you doing 90 miles in a 70-mile zone?

Chicano: I wasn't doing 90. I was going 80.

---

[30]See Trick 90.
[31]You get called "Mister" ever so often in life.

Patrolman, as he quickly stiffens and begins to flush like a sunburnt tourist: Are you gettin' smart with me?

Chicano: No. You said 80 awhile ago, now you're saying 90. I was only going 80.

Patrolman, as he pulls open the door: Get out. You calling me a liar?

Chicano, as he sees another patrolman lurching out of patrol car: No. I thought you said 80 at first. That's why I said 80, not 90.

Second Patrolman: What's the trouble? This boy been drinking? He givin' you trouble?

Chicano: No. No trouble. I ain't drunk, just a couple of beers.

First Patrolman: Boy, you are in trouble. Drunk driving, resisting arrest, disorderly conduct, disturbing the peace, 100 in a 70-mile zone. Do we take you in or you sign here?

Second Patrolman: This is not a plea of guilty, you *comprende*, amigo? This is a statement that you promise to appear in court within ten days.

First Patrolman: You in there (as he looks into the other faces). Any of you got a license? Get in behind this wheel and drive for this boy. We're taking him in right now.

Second Patrolman: Drive friendly, you hear!

Law and Order Category

Trick Number 103: Plead Guilty and Get Three

The records of prosecutors are the makings of a politician striving for a judgeship. The more offenders against society the prosecutor is able to jail, the more of a hero he becomes to the local citizenry. Deals are worked out between judge, prosecutor, and defender, in too many criminal cases.

The defense attorney, to earn a good fee for little work, is eager to work out a deal and plead his client guilty. The prosecutor is eager to get another guilty plea entered in the record and will work out a deal. The judge, being the chief administrator of justice, is not the one to stand in the way of judicial progress. By God, if the defense and prosecution both agree on the guilt and punishment, why should the judge interfere? What more open, democratic, humane, and equitable justice can be found?

All are happy except the convict, who was told he faced two to ten years for the crime he was charged with and could get three if he pled guilty with chances for parole after one year.

Media Category

Trick Number 104: What Did He Say?

It seems a conspiracy on the part of newspaper editors to send monolingual reporters (English only) to Chicano rallies. The reporter, upon arrival, soon figures out that he doesn't know what's happening, much less what is being said. He adopts a Chicano interpreter.

All you hear is: What did he say? Why'd they clap? What's so funny? How do you spell his name?

The next day you read on the last page about a rally in the paper, but figure it wasn't the one you attended.

Funny, though, the place and speakers were the same.

Media Category

Trick Number 105: What's Happening, Shee-cane-no?

The reporter in Trick 104 covers a few Chicano events. He's now an expert on Chicano affairs.

You have stopped calling on his paper to cover your activities, but he shows up from time to time.

"Why don't you call me when you're going to have a rally?" he asks. "How do you expect to get some publicity if you don't call me?" he begs. "Don't you people understand that we're on your side?" he proudly announces.

"*Chinga tu madre, cabrón,*[32]" you say.

"I'm sorry, I don't understand. What did you say?"

---

[32]For a translation, consult your local Chicano. And duck.

Media Category

Trick Number 106: The Three-Question Polka

Our ace reporter in 104 and 105 begins to get bitter because Chicanos are too dumb to understand he's trying to help. They, he reasons, are racists in reverse.

He can sure fix them in a hurry:

In a demonstration, picket line, meeting, or wherever Chicanos are gathered for action, the reporter will pick three or four persons to question.

Reporter to first person: What does your group want?

Reporter to second person: Some people have said your group is interested only in health. Is that correct? What does your group really want?

Reporter to third person: Two of your members, I can't remember their names right now, said this meeting was to protest the education of Chicanos. Are you really protesting education or against the high standards of colleges?

Reporter to fourth person: I've been here for over an hour and have talked to many of your people. Apparently, there is a wide range of interests and ideas here. Would you say that your group has much to do and little to do it with?

Fourth person: Yes. Man, we're trying to do a lot. I don't know what we're doing sometimes. We do a lot.

Later that evening, when all your friends are watching the news:

"And finally, friends, today a group of protesters picketed the entrance to our new medical school. This reporter went to the scene earlier in the day and got this eyewitness film of the events."

The film shows a couple of demonstrators smiling and posing for the camera. Your friends cheer.

"The demonstration was reported to be for 'education,' but you wouldn't guess it from talking to them. One protester said the group was protesting health, another said education, yet another said they wanted lower admission standards for Chicanos. I guess the mood of the day was reflected by the last protester we interviewed."

Your face is on the screen. Your mouth opens: "I don't know what we're doing sometimes."

Negotiation Category

Trick Number 107: Can't Have the Park

The public bodies administer public facilities. Therefore, permission to use the facilities must be granted by the administrators in charge.

You are urged caution in attempting to obtain the use of a public facility. Many a group has gone to ask for a park or hall and been turned down because "another group has it reserved for that day."

Should that happen to you once, try sending a fake inquiry about the availability of the facility before your real group applies.

Negotiation Category

Trick Number 108: Still Can't Have the Park

The administrator in charge of the public facilities gets smart after you get him once or twice.

He retaliates by telling you that confirmation will be withheld for twenty-four hours "because so-and-so also asked for the park for some group or another whose name I can't remember right now. But call me tomorrow at 10:00 a.m." Sure enough, you are informed when you call that so-and-so did call and what's-its-name was the local Fraternal Order of Wingless Dingbats.

Negotiation Category

Trick Number 109: No, You Still Can't Have the Park

You catch on to the Can't Have the Park—Part I and Part II. What can you do?

Try calling the Fraternal Order of the Wingless Dingbats and see if they are having a function. Don't expect the administrator not to have called them also. Should you succeed in proving that you are being denied access to the public facility, be careful you don't fall into Step III, that being the catch-all trick that, because of the nature of your group and the ill will it causes, you are denied: "We don't want to divide the community, you understand."

Miscellaneous Category

Trick Number 110: Some of My Best Friends Are Chicanos

Most whites and a few Spanish-surnamed Americans claim there is no discrimination. When you offer proof of very clear-cut examples of blatant prejudice, you are rebutted with many clichés, among them: "Some of my best friends are Chicanos. There is no discrimination. It's just that the banker doesn't want his daughter to marry a field hand."

Job Category

Trick Number 111: Some of My Best Friends Are Chicanos

When you push through Trick 110 and its overt discrimination model and focus on the institutional exclusion in banking, congress, publishing, medicine, judges, administrators, etc., you'll be greeted with a familiar cliché: "Some of my best friends were Chicanos. They are racists in reverse. They hate all whites and want everything given to them. Who do they think they are?"

Job Category

Trick Number 112: You're Different, Joe

Divide and conquer rules have many faces (see Trick 93). This one is the most effective trick because it is directed at a person who, if he accepts it, will on his own continue to divide his people. A Chicano is approached by his white superior[33] and told how good a worker he is, loyal, dependable, eager to learn and please. He will be told a myriad of compliments. Then the boss will place an arm around him, look José straight in the eye, and say, "Joe, I've been noticing many things about you. And you know, Joe, you're different. You really are."

You better believe José is no more. A new Joe has been born. Joe, the different Mexican.

---

[33]When Chicanos are around, there are no white inferiors, if for no other reason, we will be allowed to survive.

Political Category

Trick Number 113: He's Not Qualified[34]

It never fails that a Chicano group will get together to plan some strategy for an election and end up fielding a candidate or two. The group is enthusiastic and elated.

Then the word comes: "Is this man qualified?" Without determining criteria for answering the question, the group starts wavering in its support, and soon the campaign fizzles.

Political Category

Trick Number 114: We're for Henry B

In April 1973, the city election in San Antonio was a beautiful example of this trick. Roy Barrera was the Good Government League's[35] candidate for mayor. His opponent was Charles Becker, an ex-GGL man. During the campaign, all you could hear from gringo lips was "Vote for Barrera. He's different. He's qualified." Then Barrera was forced into a run-off, which he lost. Thank goodness.

Now all gringos claim they voted for Barrera. Had he won, it would have been a "We're for Henry B" all over again. In San Antonio, any charge of prejudice, discrimination, or racism by a Chicano against a gringo is countered by the statement, "Why, I'm not prejudiced. I'm for Henry B."

Political Category

Trick Number 115: Vote a Straight Ticket

Prior to the Raza Unida Party, few Chicanos were allowed past the primaries.[36] Now token Chicano Democrats not only are allowed to win primaries but general elections as well.

---

[34]See Trick 60 and 2.
[35]It is the political machine in San Antonio that has dominated politics since 1958.
[36]See Trick Number 62, Examples A and B.

True to form, these Chicano Democrats will campaign for themselves and the entire Democratic slate. They will ask you to vote a straight ticket for the Democratic Party.

You ask them how many times the Democratic Party has voted a straight Chicano ticket.

Political Category

Trick Number 116: Vote a Straight Ticket or Split Your Ticket

Ramsey Muñíz, the Raza Unida Party candidate for governor in 1972, was constantly plagued with the question, "What have you got against McGovern?"

Muñiz has plenty against McGovern, but during the campaign he only said that his endorsement of McGovern would come as soon as McGovern endorsed him.

How dare that Mexican ask for an endorsement!

Education Category

Trick Number 117: Mentally Retarded

Chicanitos entering school for the first time are given exams to test their proficiency of the English language.[37] To a child, almost every person I knew in the late 1940s, 1950s, and 1960s didn't perform well on the examination. In fact, very few passed the test.

Those that flunked the test were branded mentally retarded.

The exam does not make provisions for the non-English-speaking student, except in the category of retarded.

Jobs Category

Trick Number 118: Choose the Director

From time to time, a high administrative position is vacated and needs appointment. The local Chicano student groups seek to fill the position with an acceptable Chicana or Chicano.

---

[37]I have yet to find any record of English being the official language of this country.

It used to be the gringo administration would fill the slot immediately—the public is damned. Today they fill the slot after some intricate trickery—the public is damned anyway. Here's how:

The vacancy is announced and applicants sought.

An advisory committee of faculty and students[38] is appointed.

The administration slowly brings its choice out into the picture.

The local Chicano groups nominate their best choices.

The advisory committee meets and begins interviewing all the applicants.

The top administrator instructs the advisory committee to recommend their top three choices.[39]

The top administrator, after a period that gives the impression of serious study, chooses their man as director. He was number three.

The local groups wonder what happened. Their choices were numbers one and two.

Negotiation Category

Trick Number 119: Vacancies

During the years 1968 to 1971, scores of high school and junior high Chicano students protested the inferior quality of education meted to them by boycotting school. From Kalamazoo, Michigan, to Los Angeles, California, to Denver, Colorado, to San Antonio, Texas, blowouts[40] took place.

School boards of education dodged this demand with one of the oldest tricks in the book. "Can't find qualified Chicanos to teach. You find them, we'll hire them," was their slogan.

The board of education knew full well that the community groups, let alone student groups, were not prepared to search, recruit, and

---

[38]Usually such a committee is pro-administration. However, a student-dominated committee is not unheard of. Since there is more than one student organization, this gives the committee a student look.

[39]Among the "top three choices" is the pro-administration's choice. The students divided themselves among two choices and the administration forces bloc voted. (See Trick 60.)

[40]A blowout is a student walkout from school—a boycott, if you will.

attract Chicano teachers. The administration absolved themselves and placed the entire burden on the students' backs. The few Chicano teachers recruited were, of course, hired.

Soon the effort ceased. The board came out smelling like a rose, and the community or students left with their tails between their legs.

Negotiation Category

Trick Number 120: Qualified But Won't Come

A corollary to 114 is that a board of education will produce applications and copies of interviews from prospective Chicano teachers. They will announce, "Your people are being given all consideration and, in fact, your people are being sought out. But your people don't want to come to Hicksville. Your people don't want to sacrifice. Your people want big money. Your people want the big city. Your people don't want to come."

Again, the board washes its hands of the matter and you feel two inches high: Your people let you down.

Don't believe it! Ask for the names and addresses. Ask for the kind of offer made to these prospective teachers. Ask that the highest salaries be offered the Chicanos. Make the board out to be the bad guys for not hiring Chicanos when they had the chance.

Negotiation Category

Trick Number 121: It's Not in the Budget

Another demand of the numerous school blowouts was for Chicano programs: Chicano history, Chicano literature, Chicano art, and Chicano music.

The petitioned administration responded with another age-old trick: "Our interests are in the interests of students. We want these special and different programs for our Chicano students, but we must think of all students. Our school finances programs for Chinese, Greeks, Irish, Germans, Indians, Negroes, Italians, and Filipinos. It is not in the budget!"

What relevance the Chinese, Greeks, and others had to your request is left to your imagination. Wouldn't it be tremendous to learn about all those people anyway? But this is a diversionary tactic. The fact that "it is not in the budget" simply means the current operating budget. It could always be provided for in next year's budget. In fact, every school district has to amend its current budget because of additional unforeseen expenses. If they amend the budget for one expense, why not for yours?

Media Category

Trick Number 122: Can't Have the Time

During political campaigns, opposing groups use the radio and television to get their message before the public. Too many Chicano groups are easily turned away from access to the media because they are told that all the time available has been bought.

The truth of the matter is that under federal regulations, all candidates or groups must have access to the public.

Media Category

Trick Number 123: Can't Have That Time

The federal regulations also provide that all candidates and groups have the same amount of time made available and at almost the same time. In other words, the opposition can't buy up all the best time and leave you the wee hours of dawn. You also have the right to prime time.

Media Category

Trick Number 124: Can't Have Our Time

If you are in a 'geographic area where the listening audience is Chicano, your political message can be in Spanish. Call the Federal Communications Commission in Washington, if necessary, but don't let a radio or TV station tell you that a Spanish announcement can't be run during English programming.

In 1972, TV station KRGV outside of Harlingen, Texas, tried to bar the Raza Unida Party from time with all these tricks and failed. The result was either they rearranged all their political announcements to make room for us or gave us prime time. They did a little of both.

Media Category

Trick Number 125: Sorry, No Credit

When purchasing time for political advertisements in the media, remember to make your schedule in advance. Don't go at the last minute.

The stations will ask for cash up front. They are prohibited from extending credit. However, you can get around this by purchasing your time with a check dated the time your first announcement is scheduled to run. In this manner, you have the time bought and the time to raise the money.

Job Category

Trick Number 126: Too Lazy to Work

You observe that the employees in a specific business are all white. Upon inquiry, you find that the employer has never hired a Chicano. Yet, a large part of his clientele is Chicano.

Your group confronts the employer with these facts. The boss is unimpressed. He tells you that (1) he doesn't know what Chicanos are— he only hires the qualified; (2) he hired a Mexican once and he was too lazy to work; and (3) nobody is going to tell him who to hire or fire.

Job Category

Trick Number 127: No Vacancy

A smoother operator would not be as blunt as the bigot in 126. He would say that he'd think about it and pledge to hire the first qualified Chicano he can find when a vacancy occurs.

Miscellaneous Category

Trick Number 128: No Handouts

Clearly, a double standard of justice, services, education, etc., exists for Chicanos. Invariably, welfare and Chicanos are made to sound synonymous. Yet the overwhelming numbers of welfare recipients are whites. And if one adds farm subsidies to the category of federal handouts,[41] not only are most recipients white but they receive the most money.

Miscellaneous Category

Trick Number 129: Go Get an Education

The LULACs organized themselves in 1927 in Harlingen, Texas. This traditional organization has education as the panacea for Chicano social ills. As a forerunner to early childhood and bilingual education, the LULACs adopted the little school of 400. In this "school," a Chicano would learn 400 basic words in English. He then could make it.

We didn't and haven't and won't.

A thousand degrees from Harvard and speaking flawless English still will not change our status as colonial subjects.

Media Category

Trick Number 130: Edit the Editor

Newspapers depend on sensational journalism to boost their sales. Letters to the editor are a natural target for fanning racial hatred. A letter will appear that incites racial prejudice with its paternalism and covert racism. In a matter of days, irate retorts are printed, which produce more racist letters and on and on.

You write the letter to end all letters. However, when it appears in print, half of the letter is omitted and the remaining part edited. It does not read like your letter.

---

[41]Welfare is made to appear as a handout that in reality most recipients have earned with their hard-earned tax money.

You will not be the first group to begin campaign-babbles about the length of your letter, their desire to print as many as possible, apologizes for the editing, and requests to write again sometime.

Now you know that a letter to the editor must stand alone, paragraph by paragraph, and run the risk of being edited.

Media Category

Trick Number 131: More Letters to the Editor

You will not be the first group to begin a campaign of letters-to-the-editor in order to polarize a community on an issue.

Your group can use this section of the paper as effectively as the editor can.

Media Category

Trick Number 132: One Hundred Demonstrators

The media, an agent of the establishment, reports the events in a community with a biased approach. In reporting figures or numbers, the media will call on the so-called experts: police, firemen, other reporters, and the establishment representatives.

It is not unusual to read or hear that only a hundred demonstrators were present when in reality there were three hundred.

Pilón[42] Category

Trick Number 133: One Little, Two Little, Three Little . . .

Most demonstrations start on failure. A group will call for a demonstration on X day at noon. A couple of days of organizing produce fifty people on X day. However, the following day only forty show up, then thirty, then ten, until you are walking around by yourself.

All demonstrations would succeed if, instead of one big turnout and slow fizzle, the operation were reversed. Start with a few demonstrators and add ten per day.

---

[42]See Trick Number 55.

Pilón Category

Trick Number 134: Private Property

In this modern day one can hardly expect to find slavery existent. Not so with migrant families. When working for the white grower, our families must live on the property of the grower.

Take the case of the Del Monte corporation: They maintain a labor camp outside of Crystal City, Texas. In order to visit the people in the camp, you must ask permission from the camp superintendent. Should he deem your request reasonable, permission will be granted. If not, then you are barred entry. Del Monte's higher-ups claim this is to protect their property.

It took a federal court case in Michigan to determine that private property did not mean the laborers and their families.

Pilón Category

Trick Number 135: You're in the Wrong Place

In all the years of struggle, few accounts in the media have been objective, let alone biased in our favor. I confronted a stringer for *Life* magazine with this fact.

I was informed that the problem of the Chicano was quite obvious. "The news bureaus, except for Los Angeles, are not in the Southwest. The Chicano, then, is geographically in the wrong place."

Pilón Category

Trick Number 136: Bad Assignment

Ever wonder why even when Chicanos are hired, they do a poor job? The explanation is simple enough.

When a Chicano is brought on board an institution such as the media, he is given a bad assignment. Of course, he performs badly. Therefore, the performance and not the assignment now demand another poor assignment. Another poor performance, another poor assignment . . . until he quits or is fired.

Another great American theory is verified: Chicano newspapermen are inferior to white.

Pilón Category

Trick Number 137: One by One

Mass arrests were the vogue in the '60s. Few organizations learned to deal with the consequences of mass arrests, particularly the legal.

When a mass arrest was carried out on some idiotic charge, such as parading without a permit, the trials for the accused were conducted separately. Individual tricks were more expensive for the accused than the accuser. It also had the distinct advantage that the first conviction prejudiced the mind for pending cases.

Pilón Category

Trick Number 138: Suspicion of Possession

Activists effectively used political trials in the late 60s, early 70s to draw attention to their causes. However, a criminal charge prompted the political trial. Too many individuals could not reach the trial stage.

In Hondo, Texas, a Chicano candidate for the school board was charged with suspicion of possession of marijuana just prior to the election. He lost the election and the charges were dropped.

Pilón Category

Trick Number 139: Don't Vote a Full Ballot

People erroneously assume that maximum use of their voting rights demands voting in all races. This is wrong. You should vote only in those races where Chicanos are challenging.

Remember that gringos are going to bloc vote.[43] Chicanos, on the other hand, are going to vote for the most qualified.[44] For example, in the November general election, numerous public offices are up for election. Very few Chicanos appear on the ballot as candidates. If you vote for the Chicanos *and* in the other races, you give votes to the gringos needlessly; it makes the Chicanos look bad:

---

[43]Bloc voting means you vote only for your candidates.
[44]"Most qualified" means those candidates most like a gringo.

County Judge
John White (Rep.) got 70 votes (won)
Tom Anglo (Dem.) got 30 votes
County Sheriff
Gary Grey (Dem.) got 55 votes (won)
Pete Pat (Rep.) got 45 votes
County Commissioner
Bob Bibb (Dem.) got 30 votes
Jack Jones (Rep.) got 30 votes
Juan Raza (Raza Unida) got 40 votes (won)

In other words, the gringos outvoted the Chicano. Juan Raza will remember that he won barely and by a minority of the vote. Putting it another way, the majority of the people did not vote for Juan Raza. The majority of the people, however, did vote for John White and Gary Grey.

Pilón Category

Trick Number 140: You Can't Tell a Book by Its Cover[45]

Always pay attention to what's going on inside. Anytime you think you have all the tricks figured out, you are just asking for trouble. Always be alert. New tricks are being added all the time, and the gringo may come up with something extra that you didn't plan on.

Pilón Category

Trick Number 141: There's More to Come

Finally, the tricks discussed in these pages don't cover all the techniques gringos use against us now. You could never cover them all. But the next book in this series will tell about more gringo tricks and also tell about some tricks that Chicanos can use to extend our power. Watch for the next book, *The Chicano Manual on How to Handle Gringos*.

---

[45]Including this one.